To Bishop Stephen
with very best wishes.
Mark Scarlata

Petertide 2013

"Am I My Brother's Keeper?"

"Am I My Brother's Keeper?"

Christian Citizenship in a Globalized Society

MARK W. SCARLATA

CASCADE *Books* • Eugene, Oregon

"AM I MY BROTHER'S KEEPER?"
Christian Citizenship in a Globalized Society

Copyright © 2013 Mark W. Scarlata. All rights reserved. Except for brief quotations
in critical publications or reviews, no part of this book may be reproduced in any
manner without prior written permission from the publisher. Write: Permissions,
Wipf and Stock Publishers, 199 W. 8th Ave., Suite 3, Eugene, OR 97401.

Cascade Books
An Imprint of Wipf and Stock Publishers
199 W. 8th Ave., Suite 3
Eugene, OR 97401

www.wipfandstock.com

ISBN 13: 978-1-62032-462-2

Cataloguing-in-Publication data:

Scarlata, Mark W.

"Am I my brother's keeper?" : Christian citizenship in a globalized society /
Mark W. Scarlata.

xii + 158 pp. ; 23 cm. Includes bibliographical references.

ISBN 13: 978-1-62032-462-2

1. Bible. O.T. Genesis IV—Criticism, interpretation, etc.—History. 2. Globalization—Social aspects. 3. Globalization—Economic aspects. I. Title.

BS580.C3 S275 2013

Manufactured in the U.S.A.

For Bettina, Nathaniel, Madeleine, and Annabelle

Contents

Acknowledgments

THERE IS ALMOST NO end to the list of people that helped make this book possible and I regret that I will inevitably leave someone out. I am most thankful for the support and patience of my wife, Bettina, and our children Nathaniel, Madeleine, and Annabelle who have had to live with my ever-changing theology of Christian discipleship and how we practice it as a family. Over the past five years we have also enjoyed the love and support of our families while we have lived abroad. Much of this book was written following the completion of my PhD while I was at Ridley Hall, Cambridge. I am thankful for the diocese of Ely's support through our training period, for the staff at Ridley Hall, and especially for the guidance and thoughtfulness of my tutor, Adrian Chatfield. Among others who endlessly listened to my convictions were Matthias Grebe and James Orr, to whom I am grateful for their insights and friendship. I am also grateful for the comments offered by my students at St. Mellitus College. Many of the ideas for this book were engendered in a small, men's Bible study and I am thankful for each one who participated in our group and helped me form and shape some of these thoughts into a coherent whole. Finally, I would be remiss not to thank Stanwich Congregational Church and the families there that have supported us through the years. None of this would have been possible without their generosity and encouragement as we moved from pastoral ministry into the next steps of our calling.

Cambridge 2012

Abbreviations

Ant.	Josephus, *Jewish Antiquities*
ASV	American Standard Version (1901)
b.	Babylonian Talmud
CD	Karl Barth, *Church Dogmatics*
Ep.	*epistula*
ESV	English Standard Version (2001)
Gen. Rab.	Genesis Rabbah
GL	Hans Urs von Balthasar, *The Glory of the Lord: A Theological Aesthetics*
HB	Hebrew Bible
HTR	*Harvard Theological Review*
JPS	Jewish Publication Society Version of the Old Testament
JSJ	*Journal for the Study of Judaism in the Persian, Hellenistic and Roman Periods*
KJV	King James Version
LXX	The "Septuagint" Greek Version of the Old Testament
m.	Mishna
ms(s)	manuscript(s)
MT	Masoretic text
NASB	New American Standard Bible
NCV	New Century Version
NIV	The New International Version
NIrV	The New International Reader's Version
NJPS	New Jewish Publication Society Version
NKJV	New King James Version
Pesh.	Peshitta
PRE	*Pirqe de Rab Eliezer*
QG	Jerome's *Quaestiones Hebraicae in Genesim*
RSV	Revised Standard Version
SJLA	Studies in Judaism in Late Antiquity
TEV	Today's English Version
Tg. Ps.-J	Targum Pseudo-Jonathan
viz.	*videlicet*, namely
Vg	Vulgate
VT	*Vetus Testamentum*

Preface

FOR THREE YEARS I devoted myself to the study of the Cain and Abel narrative in Genesis 4:1–16 as part of my doctoral research at Cambridge University. My particular interest was not only in the original Hebrew text, but also in the ancient translations that tried to best represent this simple, yet profoundly insightful, narrative. Whenever I mentioned my area of study to others, I was confronted with a response that often went something like, "Oh yes, Cain and Abel. What do you think that story is really about?" Years later I confess that I still do not quite know! I realized however, that, like any good story, it is not necessarily about one thing in particular. Like most biblical narratives it raises a whole host of issues that human beings experience in their relationship with God and in their relationships with one another. It dredges up deep, and sometimes dark, questions about the nature of humanity and how we respond in difficult circumstances. It invites us to experience a range of emotions from sympathy, care, and mercy to hatred, violence, and judgement. And finally it asks us, as readers, to respond. The author of Genesis does not allow us to walk away from such a tragic narrative without questioning who we are, how we relate to God, and how we relate to our neighbor.

A significant portion of this book is about our response as Christians to the issues that are raised by globalization and the cultural shifts experienced by this generation. How do we relate to the "Other" in our world? Are we offering our best in worship amidst a consumer-driven society? How do we demonstrate love for our neighbor as we participate in the global economy? How do we treat the environment in a way that is pleasing to God and reflects true Christian discipleship? How do we attune our lives to the Spirit in a technological age of dislocation and wandering? Many of these questions were inspired by discussions I had regarding what it means to be a disciple of Christ in a globalized society. In all of my conversations what became apparent was that, for a Christian in the Western world, a simplistic, personalized faith that remained oblivious to the effect one's life is having across the globe is no longer possible. Instead, most conversations ended up recognizing the fact that to be a disciple of Christ meant that one had to live with both a local and global awareness in every aspect of daily life.

Every generation is responsible for rethinking what it means to be a disciple of Christ in his/her own age and this remains true for Christians today. Living in a twenty-first-century Western society that continues to be reshaped by globalization and the development of information technologies, Christians are faced with a dramatically different landscape than previous generations. We can no longer think of ourselves solely in relationship to those around us, but, rather, our relationships—and responsibilities— now extend to those throughout the entire world. Being a Christian today requires us to re-examine our lives and the choices we make in the light of those whom we might never see, yet who might be blessed—or who might suffer—because of our actions. Discipleship has not changed—Christians are still called to submit their lives fully in obedience to Christ—but as the world around us changes, we must contemplate the nature of discipleship as it practiced in the twenty-first century and how it addresses the needs of society by establishing the presence of God's kingdom through individual believers and through the wider church.

Part of this reflection will also be to explore the motifs of the Cain and Abel narrative and how they might be relevant in speaking to our contemporary context. As we walk through this story of two brothers we shall look at some of the ancient translations and traditions to see how generations of interpreters made sense of the narrative and applied it to their contemporary audiences. What did the text say to them and how did it address the issues of their day? The hope is that we might enter into a dialogue with the Scriptures, and with those who have translated and interpreted them throughout history, so that we might hear anew the good news of God's message and how it might be proclaimed afresh in our generation.

1 INTRODUCTION

Citizenship, Globalization, and Translation

THE ROMAN EMPIRE COULD arguably be considered one of the greatest civilizations in the Western world. It prided itself on technological innovation, cultural and educational superiority, and economic and military might. Rome was regarded as the eternal city and stood as the political and spiritual center of the empire. In 410 C.E., however, the city was sacked by the Visigoths, which many see as the critical point marking the decline, and ultimate fall, of the Roman Empire. It was not uncommon at the time to place the blame on Christianity—which had flourished since the reign of Constantine (c. 312–37 C.E.)—for its demise. The argument was that the abandonment of Roman deities for the Christian God angered the gods who allowed the barbarians to attack. In response to such accusations Augustine (354–430 C.E.), Bishop of Hippo, wrote one of his most valuable works on political and spiritual thought called *The City of God*.

In the light of Rome's decay and faded glory, Augustine argued that Christianity was not to blame, but, rather, there existed a fundamental cleavage between what he calls the city of God and the earthly city. The two cities exist side-by-side in the world, but they are vastly different in their values, structure, and purpose.

> And so the two cities were created by two loves: the earthly city by self-love reaching the point of contempt for God, the heavenly city by the love of God reaching the point of contempt for self. In fact, the earthly city glories in itself, the heavenly city in the Lord. While the one looks for glory from human beings, the greatest

> glory for the other lies in God, the witness of conscience. (*City of God*, 14.28)

According to Augustine each city is motivated by its "loves," or, in other words, the desires and appetites that drive them. The citizens of the city of God—i.e., Christians—are marked by their enjoyment and love of Christ, which is the only thing capable of bringing true happiness and peace on this earth. Contrary to this is the earthly city, which is founded on the love of self. These citizens are prone to seek happiness in pleasures of the flesh, in the possession of material things, in self-glorification, and in power over others. Augustine argued that the loves—or desires—of each city represent the fundamental orientation of its citizens. In the city of God people are unified by their common orientation towards love, justice, and peace, whereas the earthly city is fractured and its citizens are inclined towards narcissism, greed, and dominion.

It should be noted that, in either city, Augustine was speaking about one's orientation, or the direction in which they are heading, and not about their moral perfection. Those in the heavenly city are steering themselves towards God by trying to live in daily obedience to his commands and in submission to the Holy Spirit. They are, by no means, perfect, but they continue to alter the patterns of their lives in the hope that they will make manifest God's kingdom on earth. In the earthly city, however, one's orientation is primarily focused on the self. This does not mean that Augustine thought people in the earthly city were entirely wicked or could not perform good deeds. Rather, Augustine's emphasis is on the direction of their lives, and, in the case of the earthly city, people are pointed away from God and travelling on a path toward self-satisfaction and ultimately destruction.

Augustine believed that these two cities represented all of humanity throughout space and time and so he was able to trace the founding of the earthly city first to the rebellious angels who were consumed by pride and then to Cain who followed the angelic precedent (*City of God*, 15.5, 7). Cain was so overwhelmed by envy, and so filled with pride, that he killed his brother in an effort to establish his own power and independence. This act of fratricide functions as the dominant metaphor for the earthly city and highlights the deepest desire of those who forsake the love of God for the love of self. Pride and the lust for domination is at the heart of Cain and the citizens of the earthly city who will not rest until they have put all others beneath their feet. Their appetite for power and autonomy creates a restlessness that is never satisfied, but only promotes a never-ending cycle of conflict, death, and destruction.

Though Augustine sometimes spoke of the city of God as the church (*City of God*, 13.6), he did not believe that the two cities were visibly separated. He contended that even inside the church people were mixed together from both cities and that, throughout society, citizens of the heavenly kingdom worked alongside those of the earthly kingdom. The distinction between the two cities was, therefore, based on the direction one was traveling. Citizens of the city of God orient their lives towards the love, forgiveness and peace of Christ, while citizens of the earthly city journey towards the self and seek only the fulfillment of their own desires.

Citizens of God's kingdom, however, still struggle with sin and the temptations of power, pride, and self-absorption. Augustine spoke of sin as *aversion a Deo*—a turning away from God—whereas reconciliation and forgiveness come through *conversio ad Deum*—a turning to God. He knew that every human being has a divided will and, whether one was a Christian or not, he understood that the division and pull towards good and evil is present in every human being. The difference for citizens of the city of God is that, in Christ, they have been created anew through the Holy Spirit and now live to make his love present to all humanity through the church. Their conversion to Christ and new life within the church was not unlike the experience of changing their citizenship and devoting their allegiance to a new king. Just like Roman citizens—or converts to Roman citizenship—they would now live and act in accordance with the laws of their new country and leader. But rather than living according the lordship of Caesar, they lived according to the lordship of Christ.

The idea of citizenship in God's kingdom would have been a compelling metaphor for those living in Augustine's time. To be a citizen of Rome—particularly as a male—included a wide range of benefits from the state such as voting, owning property, having a legal marriage, the right to a trial, and the ability to preserve one's citizenship when migrating to a Roman colony. A Roman citizen could not be tortured or receive the death penalty—unless found guilty of treason—and under no circumstances could they be sentenced to death on a cross. It is no wonder that the apostle Paul appeals to his Roman citizenship in Acts 22 before being flogged without a trial and that the guards respond with fear because they had bound him illegally. Citizenship was held in the highest regard and required one to live according the laws and principles of the state in order to bring about the greatest good in society. According to Aristotle, the end goal of every community—or city-state—was to ensure the good life and happiness of its citizens (*Politics*, I.1.8–9). Thus people were encouraged to think of their lives and work as a contribution to the larger community of the state in order to bring peace and happiness to its citizens.

With the sacking of Rome, however, citizenship no longer carried the same weight and probably caused many to question their identity amidst a state in decline. As the empire crumbled, Augustine's metaphor of the city of God allowed Christians to identify the principles of citizenship with their new life and service to Christ. While still living in obedience to the laws of the state, they could shift their allegiance to live under the laws and principles of the gospel. This was not new idea, but can be heard in Paul's exhortation to the believers in Philippi as he encourages them not to be like those enemies of Christ. "But our citizenship is in heaven, and from it we await a Saviour, the Lord Jesus Christ, who will transform our lowly body to be like his glorious body, by the power that enables him even to subject all things to himself" (Phil 3:20–21).

The notion of citizenship carries with it a sense of legal obligation and one's duty to the state for the good of all its inhabitants. A citizen has privileges *and* responsibilities when living in accordance with the laws of the state. Citizens cannot pick and choose which laws they would like to follow and which ones they would rather forget about. Instead, they are subject to all the laws of the land and to the authority of its ruler. Being a citizen requires one to engage in life-long practices, to change habits, and to subject oneself to the state for the benefit of the whole community. Citizenship is not about how you feel, but it is about doing what you are required to do—whether pleasant or unpleasant—as a member of a larger community. This does not mean blind, thoughtless obedience in all instances, but it does mean that, at times, one will be required to set aside personal ambitions and preferences for the sake of benefiting the whole.

There is a communal aspect to citizenship that compels one to look beyond personal needs or desires to one's wider responsibilities to society. As a metaphor for the Christian life, therefore, it emphasizes the community (*koinōnia*) and the role—or duty—that each individual and household must play to ensure the peace and health of the wider society. Citizenship, as a model for conversion and obedience to a new Lord and a new kingdom, brings out certain nuances of the Christian life that can help us think about obedience to Christ as we live in the world today. Being a citizen in the heavenly city is not simply about reading our Bible and praying (though this is certainly critical), as if the primary goal of faith was merely nurturing our personal spirituality. Rather, it is about submitting our entire lives to the service of the king that we might usher in the peace that he desires at every level of society. This means discipleship involves not only reading Scripture and praying, but it also includes the food we eat, the clothes we buy, the investments we make, how we use our finances, the vacations we take, the way we use the Internet, the careers we choose, the time we spend with family, how we care for the poor, and so on. Far from the idea that faith is merely about an isolated personal salvation, the notion of Christian citizenship broadens the horizon of our commitment to transformation in all aspects of society and our responsibility to those in our surrounding communities, both locally and globally. Christian citizens, therefore, live not only in accordance with the laws of the state (Rom 13:1–7), but they also seek to live in obedience to the one, true king, in order to bring about the redemption and transformation of society as a whole.

Most Christians are familiar with the concept of "discipleship," and, indeed, Jesus commands his followers to go and "make disciples" of all nations (Matt 28:19). The discipleship metaphor conveys a more intimate relationship between a student and teacher. The pupil sits at the feet of the master and engages in learning through instruction and practice. To be a disciple is to be a follower and to give up one's life in order to become like one's teacher. Discipleship brings out the intimacy we share with Christ who has become our mentor, our tutor, and even dwells within us through the Holy Spirit (Rom 8). This relational aspect of faith is critical to an understanding of how we live out a life of discipleship as a follower of Christ.

Both metaphors of citizenship and discipleship are important for how we understand the nature of our faith and what it means to participate in God's kingdom. In the coming chapters, however, we shall focus on the notion of citizenship as we walk through the story of Cain and Abel. Augustine argues that Cain was the founder of the earthly city, and we shall see how the elder brother symbolizes the characteristics of its citizens. But we shall also consider the contrasting traits of those who belong to the heavenly city and, in particular, how those traits might be made manifest in Christians who live and work in today's globalized society.

For followers of Christ in Augustine's day citizenship carried distinct connotations within their local communities and within the context of a declining Roman empire. Christians today, however, are citizens in a vastly different world. Immense distances no longer separate us and we can connect with nearly anyone at any moment in time. Our personal actions no

longer affect only our local communities, but they can have global consequences. Christians are now living in a global city-state and, as citizens of
the heavenly city, are responsible to bring about a political, economic, and
social order both at home and abroad.

To be a citizen of the city of God in today's culture means that we take
seriously the rights, privileges, duties, and commandments of the gospel
so that we might usher in God's promised peace—or shalom—to a global
community that remains fraught with suffering, violence, and death. In his
work on the ministry of the church in the modern world, Pope Paul VI
exhorts Christians to recognize their citizenship in God's kingdom as it is
worked out here on earth. He commends all believers,

> to strive to discharge their earthly duties conscientiously and in
> response to the Gospel spirit. They are mistaken who, knowing
> that we have here no abiding city but seek one which is to come,
> think that they may therefore shirk their earthly responsibilities
> . . .This split between the faith which many profess and their daily
> lives deserves to be counted among the more serious errors of our
> age. (*Gaudium et Spes*, 43)

Though the citizen of the heavenly city awaits the final consummation of
God's kingdom, he or she works towards its establishment here on earth as
it is in heaven.

Yet when we speak about being a citizen of God's kingdom on earth
in the following chapters, we shall speak primarily about one's orientation.
The object of this book is not to make people feel guilty about how little
they are doing to address issues of faith and globalization, or to present
what it looks like to be the perfect, modern-day Christian. Rather, the hope
is that we will begin to wrestle with what it means to orient our lives towards Christ as citizens of his kingdom in the twenty-first century. Are we
taking steps in the right direction in our life of faith when it comes to things
like using the Internet, or wisely considering how much—and what—we
consume, or promoting justice through economic practice, or considering
our use of natural resources? As we look at these topics in more detail,
the emphasis will not be on how much—or how little—we are doing but,
rather, we shall focus our attention on the direction and bearing of our
lives as citizens in the city of God. Are we oriented toward Christ in how
we use social media? Are we taking steps towards generosity and giving
considering our consumer lifestyles? Are we aligning ourselves with justice
in our economic transactions? Are we moving towards sustainability and

communal harmony in our relationship with creation? And are we gauging our use of technology and the impact it is having our on daily lives?

All of these are not meant to be questions of accomplishment, but questions of inclination and attitude. And though there will be suggestions about specific things we might do as Christians in a globalized society, our discussion will primarily be concerned with how we comprehend our world through a biblical-theological lens and how we participate in it as members of the heavenly city. There are many excellent books on how to practice the Christian disciplines, but our primary goal will be to raise questions regarding the specific challenges believers face in a globalized society and how they might respond to those challenges.

Citizenship is about an individual's movement and reorientation towards the rules and laws that govern a particular nation or kingdom, which serve to benefit the entire community. As citizens of God's kingdom we orient our lives towards Christ, making every effort to journey in his direction and to bring about the blessing that he desires to pour out on all humanity. Sometime we take great leaps in his direction and other times we take small steps. At other moments we hopelessly fall flat on our faces! No matter how we progress, we can delight and trust in the hope that we have a new citizenship in Christ and that, as participants in his kingdom, we have the ability to bear witness to a servant-King in every aspect of our lives. So as we walk through the story of Cain and Abel and listen to interpreters and voices from the past, the hope is that we can see afresh what it means to be a citizen of God's kingdom in the twenty-first century and how we might continue to reorient our lives to Christ in the light of a globalized society.

The City of God on a Global Scale

Augustine perceived the city of God as a kingdom that stretches throughout time to all ages and all places, incorporating the whole of the human race, so he might not have been surprised by the fairly recent phenomena of globalization. The term "globalization" has taken on various nuances, but its most basic definition refers to the integration of the world's population socially, economically, and politically. Though the term is commonly used in reference to economic internationalization—and is often synonymous with global capitalism—in this discussion we shall use a much broader definition, which, at a minimum, describes the phenomena of being interconnected with other people throughout the globe. While there are important opinions regarding the effects of globalization (e.g., economic injustice, poverty, or ecological destruction), which we shall discuss in later chapters, the focus for now will be on the more general phenomena of cultures being integrally connected worldwide.

Globalization, as experienced today, has contributed to events that would likely not have taken place a couple of generations ago. A recent example is the "credit crunch" of 2007, where we witnessed widespread destruction, both financially and socially, that was, in part, due to the increased unification of the world's economies. Through the development of communication and information technologies we are socially and culturally interconnected on a level unlike any previous society. The uprisings of the "Arab Spring" demonstrate the power of these technologies even to help engender cultural and political revolution. With the rapid exchange of ideas, events, and popular culture, there has been a significant shift in how we understand our place within the world and how we are to respond to increased interconnectedness. Some have reacted by rejecting globalization, others have remained indifferent, while others have wholeheartedly embraced it. However we choose to respond, globalization is not something that can be ignored.

The growing convergence of cultures, however, also opens up vast opportunities for expressing the gospel throughout the world. Remarkably, this can be done by travelling to foreign nations or by sitting in front of our computers. Yet with our increased integration, we are also laden with growing responsibility. No longer are we only obligated to love our neighbor in our local communities—those we can physically see, touch, and hear—but we now have the opportunity to extend love to others throughout the world on a daily basis. Consequently, whereas it is easier to discern when I have injured or hurt someone who is physically present in my life, I must now be conscious that my local actions might have a positive or negative effect on my neighbors throughout the globe. The social, economic, and political integration of people throughout the world presents new challenges for the modern Christian. And one way we might begin to address these issues is to pause and meditate on the answer to Cain's simple—yet penetrating—question that so easily falls from his cynical lips: "Am I my brother's keeper?" (Gen 4:9)

The answer to this question is obviously a resounding "Yes!" At least that is likely the answer the author of Genesis wants us to cling to throughout the rest of the book as we are confronted with the discord between Isaac and Ishmael, Jacob and Esau, and Joseph and his brothers. We are, in fact, our brother's keeper, or, to use language more appropriate to our contemporary context, we are meant to care for and to "keep" our neighbor. And our neighbor, as Jesus taught, is every human being who has been created in the image of God. Cain's impertinent question after murdering Abel has challenged generations upon generations of Jews and Christians alike, and it now challenges us to re-examine how we are caring for and "keeping" our neighbor in the midst of a modern globalized society. If the earthly city was founded on pride, envy, and murder, how will we establish the heavenly city in the twenty-first century with humility, love, reconciliation, and care for our brothers and sisters throughout the world?

In previous generations caring for our neighbor might have meant tending to the needs of the old woman who lives down the street, or a co-worker, or the people next to us in the pews or on the streets. While those in our local communities still deserve our utmost love and attention, there is also a neighbor who lives in the global South who may be adversely affected every time we buy a cup of coffee. There is a neighbor who lives in India or Asia that may remain in poverty because of the clothes we purchase. There may be a neighbor in Africa suffering because of the way we have treated the environment. It is somewhat terrifying to know what we do as individuals in our local communities can, and will, have global consequences whether positive or negative. Christians cannot, therefore, be content with a faith that is merely concerned with one's own self-interests or personal spirituality without recognizing that, at this unprecedented moment in history, the human race is intricately bound together socially, politically, and economically. Far from the world of the Genesis author, our brother and sister is connected to us on a global scale, but care for them is still, nonetheless, essential.

Since rapid global changes are increasingly part of our everyday lives, regardless of whether we think of these as positive or negative, the church has the opportunity to employ the fluidity of modern communication and integration to shape the moral and ethical path the world takes into the future. Pope John Paul II writes, "No system is an end in itself, and it is necessary to insist that globalization, like any other system, must be at the service of the human person; it must serve solidarity and the common good."[1] If we think of globalization as the system of integration that defines our contemporary society, then we can begin to contemplate how, as citizens of God's kingdom, we can use the tools and constructs of this phenomena

1. Pope John Paul II, "Papal Address to Academy of Social Sciences," 27 April 2001.

9

to bring justice to the poor and to love and care for our neighbor. In the coming chapters we shall address some of the specific issues globalization raises, but for now we shall turn to another aspect of this book, which is the translation and transmission of the Bible and its use in our interpretation today.

TRANSLATION AND TRANSMISSION: HEARING THE VOICES OF THE PAST

The Old Latin biblical texts Augustine used for his study would have sounded somewhat different to our modern English translations. In fact, many of the church fathers—and other ancient interpreters—would have read Bibles that had slight variations in their translations, as the texts were copied and communicated from one language to another over the centuries. And while today's technologies offer the rapid—and sometimes instantaneous—communication of thoughts and ideas across the globe, the problem of how best to translate those ideas so that they contain the same force and appropriate meaning in other languages and cultures still exists. In the ancient world, on a more localized level, people faced similar challenges of how to translate and communicate other traditions—in this case, the Bible—into their own cultural contexts so that it remained true to the original text but also made sense in their language.

In the third century (B.C.E.) Jews who were brought up in Alexandria (Egypt) wanted to read the Scriptures in their native tongue, and so the first five books of the Bible (or "Torah") were translated into Greek from the original Hebrew. At other points in history Aramaic was adopted as the common language for Jews (and others) around Palestine and so in Jesus's day it is likely that Aramaic translations were read alongside the Hebrew in the synagogues, so that the average person might understand. Later on, with rise of the Roman Empire, the Latin version emerged through the translations of Jerome and held prominence in the church up until the time of the Reformation. Today we find ourselves marking the four hundredth anniversary of the Authorized (King James) Version and its unprecedented impact on the English-speaking world. Like others before them, the King James translators wanted to produce an accurate rendering of the Bible for the culture of their day.

In our age of technological advances we now have an over-abundance of English translations, which makes it difficult for some to imagine a time when the Bible was only read in Latin by those who were fortunate enough to have an education. Yet for most people living prior to the Reformation, having a translation of the Bible in their native tongue would have been a luxury. At a time when English Bibles are so readily available in so many versions there might be a tendency to forget that we—as English speakers—are, in fact, reading a translation of something that emerged from an ancient world whose cultures and languages are vastly different than our own. When we come to interpret the Bible it is, therefore, healthy to step back from the plethora of English versions that surround us and think, for a moment, about what goes into the work of translation and how that affects the reading of the text we have before us today.

In his preface to the 1611 edition of the King James Version, Miles Smith, one of the translators, eloquently states that:

> Translation it is that openeth the window, to let in the light; that breaketh the shell, that we may eat the kernel; that putteth aside the curtain, that we may look into the most Holy Place; that removeth the cover of the well, that we may come by the water, even as Jacob rolled away the stone from the mouth of the well...Indeed, without translation into the vulgar tongue, the unlearned are but like children at Jacobs well (which was deep) without a bucket or some thing to draw with.

With a series of metaphors tied to scriptural motifs, Smith is able to convey something that we, in our contemporary world, may have forgotten—translation is what gives us the ability to dip deeply into the well and drink from the cold, subterranean streams of God's Word.

Swamped by the vast number of English translations on the market, it would be easy to think that the Bible just somehow appeared in English one day, by God's providence, and that was it. Years before I studied Greek and Hebrew I never really thought about my Bible as a translation and, to be honest, I am not sure that I could have named the original biblical languages! Yet the more that I studied the different translations—both ancient and modern—I realized that, when reading my English Bible, it was very tempting to think of Scripture as emerging from one culture and one language when in fact the Bible is very much a multilingual and multicultural book.

The Hebrew of the Old Testament comes from a Jewish culture in the ancient Near East spanning hundreds of years. They spoke about God in particular ways, they worshiped God by offering sacrifices at altars, the tabernacle, the temple—and even on the high places when they were not supposed to!—and they composed songs and prayers for different festivals and seasons throughout the year. They were surrounded by the competing religions and worldviews of their Egyptian, Assyrian, and Babylonian neighbors. The Aramaic in the Bible—mainly in Daniel and Ezra—comes from the post-exilic period when Persian culture dominated the Near East. The Greek of the New Testament stems from a very different Greco-Roman culture that had its own religion, art, and philosophy, which often spoke of God in more abstract language. In Greek thought one might refer to God as omnipotent or omnipresent, whereas in the Hebrew one might speak about God as the mighty warrior, king, or the faithful shepherd. The Bible is, therefore, a text that emerges from various cultures and languages that has been interpreted through the work of translators who, with every good intention, strive to bring to light that which remains in the shadows and in the depths of "Jacob's well." Thus it is important to remember that we are reading Scripture—in the English language—through the lens of the translator(s).

This does not mean that the English versions we have today are inaccurate or somehow misleading. In fact, the sheer number of translations indicates that no one version gets it right, so to speak, and that there is a continued need to reinterpret texts in each new generation. Translation of the Scriptures engenders humility and as readers of translations we need to approach the text with a certain amount of humility ourselves. It is truly amazing to think that God does not privilege one language or culture to convey his Word. Though it has been claimed by some,[2] there is no singular "holy tongue" through which God communicates his message. The example of Pentecost demonstrates his blessing upon all languages as vehicles for the message of the gospel. Later in his preface, Smith goes on to address this issue of accuracy in translation and concludes that no matter what the possible word variations, Scripture is clear and consistent when dealing in all matters of faith, hope, and charity. So while we have an incredibly accurate text before us, it is, in some ways, provisional. The translator knows that no single voice can render a "perfect" version of the Bible, but, instead, he or she invites us to explore an ancient world where God reveals himself in various degrees through creation, the prophets, and through his Son,

---

2. The pseudepigraphic book Jubilees (12:15–26) tells the story of how when God opened the mouth of Abraham he began to speak in Hebrew, which was the tongue of the original creation that had ceased since Babel. The rabbis also told stories about humanity's original language. "Rabbi Judah in the name of Rab said, 'The first man spoke Aramaic'" (b. Sanh. 38b).

Jesus Christ. This unveiling continues today as God is revealed through the Scripture and through his church.

What, then, is the work of the translators? In Smith's words, they open the window, crack the shell, or draw back the curtain. It is the work of revelation—bringing to light that which remains obscure. In this case, it is the ancient languages of the text that are unfamiliar to the average person and so these ancient words, which come out of their own particular cultural context, must be rendered with appropriate meaning into different languages amidst the various cultural contexts of our world today. Without diving too deep into various linguistic theories, at its most basic level, a translation will do one of two things; it will either bring the reader to the original text, or it will bring the original text to the reader. The prior might be a translation that is more stilted and follows the grammar and syntax of the original language, which often sounds foreign and disturbing in the target language—in this case, English. For example, Young's Literal Translation (YLT) of Gen 2:18 reads, "And Jehovah God saith, 'Not good for the man to be alone, I do make to him an helper—as his counterpart.'" While this closely follows the Hebrew syntax, it does not sound particularly pleasing to the ear. A translation that seeks to capture the sense of the passage will render the original text with the target language and audience in mind. Take the same verse above in the NIV: "The LORD God said, 'It is not good for the man to be alone. I will make a helper suitable for him.'" The result is a translation that reads smoothly, uses relevant vocabulary, and connects with readers as if the text was originally written in their own language. Let us look at a few other examples from the Old Testament.

There is an idiom in biblical Hebrew for anger that can be translated literally as "his nose became hot." The phrase can be used to describe human anger, as in Genesis 30:2 where Jacob is angry with Rachel, or it can describe God's anger like in Exodus 4:14 where he is frustrated with Moses's less than enthusiastic response to his calling. Now listen to how this would sound in English if translated literally:

And Jacob's nose became hot against Rachel . . . (Gen 30:2)

Then the LORD's nose became hot against Moses . . . (Exod 4:14)

Most of the modern English versions translate with "his anger burned," or "his anger was kindled," to give the idiom a meaning that we can easily understand. Since the language is familiar to us, we do not have to think about what the original text actually says. But if the translations above were used, it would cause us to pause and think about what was written in the original. This is what is meant by saying a translation either brings the reader back to the original or brings the original to the reader.

Another example of a difficult text will help illustrate how we read through the lens of a particular translation. In Exodus 33:11 we are told that Moses, unlike anyone else, spoke to God "face-to-face" as if speaking to an old friend. Later in the same chapter, however, Moses asks God to show him his glory but the Lord responds, "You cannot see my face, for man shall not see me and live" (Exod 33:20). In both instances the Hebrew uses the word *panim* for "face," but this presents the striking paradox of Moses being able to see God's face at one moment, but not being able to see God at another. To get around this apparent contradiction, the Greek translator uses the adjective *enōpios* in v. 11, which can mean "in the presence of," and could be translated, "And the Lord spoke to Moses in his very presence." In v. 20, however, the translator then uses *prosopon* ("face"), which is used to describe someone's physical face. The subtle change in the text, however, allows for the passages to exist side-by-side without an evident contradiction.

Some of the Aramaic Targum translations resolve the difficulty by saying that Moses spoke to God "speech with speech" but that God would not let him see his "Shekhinah" glory. In this instance the addition of the "Shekhinah" makes clear that Moses could not see the visible presence of the Lord associated with God's coming down on Mt. Sinai, or the "cloud" that filled the tabernacle and later the temple. Exodus 33 is an excellent example of the biblical author's wrestling with how to describe the intimate nature of Moses's relationship with the Lord while still maintaining the profound mystery of how a finite human might approach the infinite, almighty, transcendent, and wholly other God. In this instance, the translators do their best to interpret and resolve the apparent paradox in the original text.

Let us briefly look at a New Testament example that has more to do with how translation might be influenced by social or political factors. When the great reformer William Tyndale set out to translate the Bible into English he came across the word *ekklesia* in the Greek, which means an assembly of people. In the New Testament context, however, this most often refers to the Christians who gathered together to meet and pray. In most English versions today the word is translated as "church," but during Tyndale's time the word "church" carried with it a host of baggage tied to centuries of Catholic authority. So rather than upholding the notion that Scripture supports the institutional structure of the Catholic Church,

Tyndale, instead, translated *ekklesia* with "congregation" and provided re-
formers with further biblical grounding that upheld their practices of alternative expressions of worship and life in the church. Interestingly, the King
James Version, which was tied to the authority of the monarchy in England,
decided to keep the word "church," probably because of the political and
institutional nuance that it carried.

In a lecture celebrating the anniversary of the Authorized Version,
Archbishop Rowan Williams writes, "Rather than nailing down or exhausting the essential meaning of an 'original', translation intensifies and extends
that meaning."[3] This is not to say we are simply awash in a sea of interpretation where the original text can mean anything we want it to mean.
The "plain meaning" of the biblical text and its truths can be rendered
adequately, but on top of this foundation stands a world of living words
that must be interpreted and reinterpreted in different cultures for each
generation. Williams goes on to say that we do not have "a provisionality
of vagueness or anarchy, rather an everlasting and incurable uncertainty
as to whether the adequate word has been found for meanings that exceed
what any one tongue might say and are constantly generating fresh layers of significance."[4] With his typical eloquence Williams identifies what
is so critical in understanding any biblical text in one's own tongue—no
one person or language can sum up the depth of meaning or importance
of the Scriptures, and that there remains an interpretive process that will
always be searching for words commensurate in meaning to the original,
which shed new light on the truth contained therein. The message of Scripture is plain, but only as words are unveiled from their ancient context and
brought into the light of contemporary culture and language can we begin
to understand their significance as they relate to us today.

Because Scripture contains these layers of meaning that have the potential to address any particular milieu, I believe that the narrative of Genesis 4 can be looked at though fresh eyes as we question what it means to
be a Christian citizen amidst the globalized and consumer-driven culture
of our day. The themes it contains speak to how we relate to God, to one
another, to the church, and to our environment. Yet as we read the biblical
text we listen to it alongside translators and interpreters who, throughout
the centuries, have wrestled with how best to render this narrative for their
own audiences. So we shall proceed by examining the Cain and Abel story

3. Williams, "'Cloven Tongues,'" paragraph 8.
4. Ibid.

while hearing the voices of the faithful who have gone before us, in the hope that it might shed light on the truth of God's Word as it speaks to today's culture.

The Ancient Texts

What are the ancient versions of the Bible and where did they come from? Since many are unfamiliar with the different ancient translations and interpretations of the Bible, the following section will give a brief summary and definition of terms used throughout the book. If the terms below seem like a lot to digest in one sitting, you can always skip over them now and refer back to these pages as you read through the rest of the book.[5]

LXX (Septuagint): The term "Septuagint" refers to the original translation of the first five books of the Bible (i.e., the Pentateuch), but more generally refers to the oldest Greek renderings of the Hebrew Bible, which occurred from the third century (B.C.E.) onwards. The Roman numeral "LXX" (=70) is used to signify the Greek translations since it refers to the seventy translators that worked on the text. The story about the events that took place surrounding the translation are found in a document called the *Letter of Aristeas,* which tells of how Ptolemy II (ca. 280 B.C.E.), the king of Egypt, commissioned the work for his great library. Some dispute the historical authenticity of the letter, but, whatever the reason for its creation, the LXX was a monumental undertaking without precedent in the Hellenistic world. For the first time Greek-speaking Jews in Alexandria could read the Scriptures in their own tongue. This translation also had a significant impact on the writing of the New Testament, since most of its authors tended to quote from the LXX rather than the Hebrew. The apostle Paul, who himself was a Pharisee and would have been proficient in Hebrew, cites the LXX in over half of his quotations from the Old Testament. It is likely that the New Testament authors would have known both versions, but, since Greek was the common language of Jesus's day, the LXX was the preferred text especially for the Greek-speaking Gentiles.

The Targums: The Targums are translations of the Hebrew Bible into Aramaic that were used orally in the synagogue. The use of the Targums were strictly monitored by rabbinic laws. One rule stated that, in the synagogue,

---

5. Unless otherwise noted, all translations of the ancient versions are my own.

the Targum was to be recited from memory after Scripture had been read so that it did not appear that the speaker was reading from the actual Hebrew Bible, which was the authoritative source. It is unclear whether the Targum translations originated as liturgical readings, but some point in Nehemiah 8 when Ezra read from the book of the law and it was "explained clearly" to those in the congregation. Many take this to mean that the Hebrew was simultaneously being translated into Aramaic, which was the vernacular of the Jews in Palestine at that time. We cannot be sure that this was the start of the Targum tradition but it does demonstrate that, at a critical time in the history of God's people (during the rebuilding of the temple) the Scriptures needed to be translated into the common language of the day.

Though the noun *targum* contains the basic sense of "translation," the rabbinic Hebrew verb can also mean "explain." The role of the targumist was not merely to offer a translation, but to provide a version of the Hebrew that gave an explanation of the passage especially when the text was difficult. Think of it as a Hebrew Bible with officially stamped study notes placed within the text itself! Because the rabbis controlled what did or did not go into a Targum, it was, in some ways, a translation *and* interpretation together with the official rabbinic seal of approval. What is unique about the Targums is that, because the text was meant to be read alongside the original Hebrew, the translators could take liberties with the biblical texts and, in attempts to make them more culturally relevant, could include expansions that reflected their own particular religious or theological concerns. Yet despite these expansions, the translators took their work very seriously, which is reflected in the instructions of a rabbi to a scribe: "Be attentive to your work, for your craft does the work of Heaven. Should you omit a single letter or add a single letter, you will destroy the entire world."[6]

Many Christians who are unfamiliar with this tradition of translation and interpretation often dismiss it as merely fanciful and feel it has little to do with what the Bible actually says. It is important, however, to remember that alongside the Bible there have always been interpretations and stories that might not necessarily be "true," but they are there to help make sense of the biblical texts. Oftentimes the Bible is silent when we want it to speak, and when the text is difficult to understand we do our best to "explain clearly" its meaning. The Targums are, therefore, like a vast treasury of Jewish interpretation that represent generations of faithful believers who sought to understand, and to make known, the riches and mysteries found within the

6. *b. Erub.* 13a.

Hebrew Bible. The Targums we have today were compiled over centuries after the life of Christ and though they did not have the authority of the Hebrew text, their importance for the Jewish community was considerable and remains so to this day.

The Peshitta (Syriac): The translation of the Bible into Syriac is probably the least known among Western Christians today, but it has an important role in the history of biblical translation and early church tradition. Syriac is a dialect of Aramaic and was the primary language of many early churches as Christianity spread throughout the Middle East, India, and Asia minor. There is some question about the origins of the Old Testament in Syriac and whether it was originally translated by Jews or Christians. Either way, it is likely that the translations took place in the city of Edessa (in modern day Turkey) no later than 200 C.E. The version is called the "Peshitta," which means "simple" or "common." Like the Vulgate (Latin), the goal was to take the biblical text and make it available in the common language of the day. Yet, like the other versions, the Peshitta translated the Hebrew and Greek into a particular culture at a specific time in history. It reveals a tradition that is much closer to the Semitic side of Christianity and throughout this book we will look at commentaries from some of the prominent Syrian church fathers, such as Ephrem and Aphrahat.

The Vulgate: While we know very little about the translators of the other versions, such is not the case with the Latin Bible translated by Jerome (c. 347–420 C.E.). During Jerome's lifetime the Bible had already been translated into Old Latin, but this was an assortment of texts that were essentially renderings of the LXX. And while Jerome often used the LXX in his work, his goal was to produce a Latin text that was faithful to the original Hebrew. Jerome was well aware of the complexities of rendering the biblical text into Latin and defended his method of translating in a let-ter to his friend: "For I myself not only admit but freely proclaim that in translating from the Greek (except in the case of the Holy Scriptures where even the order of the words is a mystery) I render sense for sense and not word for word."[7] Over a thousand years later Martin Luther, facing similar criticisms, wrote about translating a passage from John 6: "But I would rather forsake the German language than deviate from the Word."[8] Despite Jerome's comments on the superiority of translating "sense for sense," he was forced to find a balance between his role as translator and interpreter

7. Jerome, *Ep.* 51.

8. Luther, "Sendbrief vom Dolmetschen," 164.

when rendering biblical texts and, as his commentaries demonstrate, he often struggled with how to best achieve this in the Latin. His effort to translate the Bible in the *vulgar* language of his day demonstrates, once again, the challenges every translator faces when trying to make Scripture relevant in a particular culture at a particular time.

The Talmud: The Talmud is not a biblical translation, but since many Christians are not familiar with it, and since we will hear from several ancient rabbis throughout this book, I thought it would be worthwhile to give a brief summary of this vast collection of rabbinic sayings that has shaped the Jewish religion for centuries. The word *talmud* means "study" or "learning" and refers to the teachings a student would acquire from his or her teacher. The Talmud is comprised of two collections of rabbinic commentary (one from Palestine and the other from Babylonia [modern Iraq]) that has become the core of Jewish legal and moral belief. Both the Palestinian Talmud and the Babylonian Talmud are compilations of rabbinic sayings that include all types of material including biblical interpretation, legal instruction, stories, anecdotes, and the like. The majority of the text is concerned with explaining and interpreting an earlier rabbinic collection of writings called the Mishnah. The Mishnah is another compilation of rabbinic writings that attributes its legal regulations and beliefs about Judaism to about 150 authorities that lived anywhere between 50–200 C.E. Some of these were rabbis who lived before the destruction of the temple by the Romans in 70 C.E., others lived through the bar-Kokhba revolt in 132–35 C.E., while others lived at the time of its writing. It is thought to contain authoritative and binding explanations of the Hebrew Bible and, in Jewish theology, serves as a complement and supplement to the Scriptures, especially when legal materials from the Pentateuch are unclear.

It might be difficult for some Christians to consider a commentary on the Bible as having the same authority as the Bible itself, but this has been the case for the Jewish faith following the New Testament period. And while we will not have much interaction with the Mishnah in this book, we will be looking at some of the rabbinic comments in the Talmud, which, for some Jews today, still represent the orthodox teaching of the faith. As a Christian, we can certainly put aside these rabbinic interpretations if we wish, but I would suggest we not be so quick to dismiss the voices of the past before we have heard how they might speak to us in the present.

Having briefly touched on some of the issues surrounding biblical translation, and having heard from some of the KJV translators themselves, it is somewhat ironic that in certain Christian circles today there is tenacious defense of the KJV as being *the* authorized English Bible. The very translators themselves, especially Miles Smith, did not claim irrefutable correctness for the translation, nor did they appeal to the orthodoxy—or Christian morality—of the translators themselves as a sign of the quality of their work. Instead, they understood that the final authority of Scripture lies not in one particular translation, but from the continued practice of shared discernment in its reading under the guidance of the Holy Spirit within the body of Christ. Thus, as we approach the translations of the Cain and Abel narrative, we can, with open ears, hear the voices of both past and present to help us understand this profound story in the light of our own culture and the globalized world in which we live.

We shall proceed, therefore, with the fitting advice of Ephrem the Syrian as we examine this ancient story of Cain and Abel that has captivated the minds of interpreters throughout the centuries:

> He [God] has hidden in his word all kinds of treasures so that each
> one of us, wherever we meditate, may be enriched by it. . . . There-
> fore, whoever encounters one of its riches must not think that he
> has found all that is in it, but [rather] that it is this alone that he is
> capable of finding from the many things within it.[9]

9. *Commentary on Tatian's Diatessaron* 1.18–19.

2 Hospitality and the Other

Breaking Bread in a Virtual World

Now Adam knew Eve his wife, and she conceived and bore Cain, saying, "I have gotten a man with the help of the LORD." And again, she bore his brother Abel. Now Abel was a keeper of sheep, and Cain a worker of the ground.

—GENESIS 4:1–2

ONE OF THE GREAT challenges the twenty-first-century Christian faces is the rapid growth of information and communication technologies. While there may be a few who shy away from mobile phones and the Internet, the majority of our world is now connected in ways that were impossible fifty years ago. Yet with the vast advancements in our capability to "connect" with one another, we also recognize how the changing shape of communication is affecting our ability to relate to one other face-to-face. If you sit down at a café in many places you will often see more people staring into a glowing screen than paying attention to the person sitting opposite them. Yet despite all of our technological advances we are still human beings with the capacity to hate or to love, to kill or to give life, to exclude or to embrace through these new tools that we have at our disposal. The virtual world now offers us an arena to extend the love of Christ to others, but it also affords us the opportunity to trivialize relationships or shut out others from community.

I recently read of a high school student who suffered from so much mental and emotional abuse on Facebook that she committed suicide, and occurrences such as these will, no doubt, become more frequent in our age of social networking. There are clever ways that we can now electronically exclude others, whether in chat groups, on social networking sites, or through other forms of communication. People can destroy the lives and reputations of others by text or by posting sexually explicit pictures online as an act of spite or retribution. Even a mistaken—or intentional—tweet or video can go viral in a matter of minutes and be shared by millions of people. In some ways, our capacity to destroy peoples' lives, to malign them, and to cast them as Other has become dangerously simple in our age of communication. What happens online can be immediately shared throughout the world, and the suffering of the individual victim can be exponentially magnified under the weight of global scrutiny. Christian citizens of the twenty-first century are, therefore, faced with an entirely new medium where relationships can be nurtured or destroyed. Social networking and online communities offer new venues to connect to others and to offer hospitality, but there is also a darker side that cannot go unaddressed by citizens of the heavenly city. In chapter 6 we shall discuss more in depth the potential effects of social networking as it relates to identity formation, but, for the moment, we shall look at it in the context of community and hospitality. Let us turn, then, to the birth of Cain—and to the larger Genesis narrative—to see how this ancient story of two brothers might speak to our treatment of others and how we might care for our global neighbor through the technology afforded to us today.

The many interpretive traditions surrounding the birth story of Cain range from normal conception to sexually illicit affairs. Almost every English translation conveys the simple birth of Adam and Eve's first son. There is, however, a tricky grammatical issue in the Hebrew at the end of Eve's declaration that could be interpreted in different ways. Most English versions have something like, "I have acquired a man with the help of the LORD," and the same is true for most of the ancient versions. If we translated the Hebrew literally, however, it could read, "I have acquired a man, the LORD," or possibly, "I have acquired a man *with* the LORD." There are two things that stick out here: why would Eve say that she had acquired, or gotten, a "man" rather than a "son" or a "child"? And what does it mean that she acquired "the LORD," or possibly "a lord"? It is certainly a strange statement to say the least and was obscure enough to engender a host of traditions regarding Cain's birth. When Martin Luther produced the final revision of his German Bible in 1545, he translated the verse, "I have the

man, of the LORD." Luther believed that Eve understood her accomplishment as giving birth to the promised seed of Gen 3:15 where God states:

> I will put enmity between you and the woman,
> and between your offspring and her offspring;
> he shall bruise your head,
> and you shall bruise his heel.

Thus Eve thought that Cain would fulfill God's word by being the one who
would bruise the serpent's head. This understanding is entirely possible
from the Hebrew, but there was another interpretive tradition that was
much more diabolical in tone that can be found in both Jewish and Christian interpretation over the centuries.

One of the Targum translations that we shall look at in the coming
chapters is called Pseudo-Jonathan (Tg. Ps.-J.) and it retells the opening of
the narrative in a decidedly different manner. It translates Gen 4:1–2:

> And Adam knew his wife Eve, who had conceived from Sammael,
> the angel of the Lord. And again, from her husband Adam, she
> gave birth to his twin sister and to Abel. And Abel was a shepherd
> of flocks and Cain was a man tilling the earth.

The expansions in the Targum may contain the earliest identification of
Cain as the offspring of the angel Sammael (= Satan). One reason for this
development was possibly because of the description of Seth's birth in Gen
5:3:

> When Adam had lived 130 years, he fathered a son in his own
> likeness, after his image, and named him Seth.

We notice that the author of Genesis emphasizes the fact that Seth was
fathered after Adam's own "likeness" and "image." The language clearly
echoes the original creation of humanity in Gen 1:26 and, since this phrase
was not used to describe Cain, this may have contributed to the idea that
the firstborn son was unnaturally conceived. There are other extra-biblical
accounts of Eve having been sexually seduced by the serpent, which may
also have contributed to this translation, but it appears that the motivation
behind the Targum rendering of Gen 4:1 stemmed from the difficult text, as
well as from the desire to illuminate extra-biblical traditions. In this interpretation Eve is seen in the light of her moral deterioration in the garden,
which is marked by the birth of Cain, the murderer. We discover that Cain

was not the true son of Adam, but was the outcome of Eve's sexual relations with a heavenly being.

Other rabbinic and Jewish apocryphal works also express the idea that Eve was impregnated by Satan. One of the rabbis commented, "When the snake had sexual relations with Eve, he pumped her up with passion."[1] The Jewish apocryphal literature contains the earliest Greek writing that reflects the tradition of Eve's seduction. In a series of books called Maccabees— which you will find today in Catholic Bibles, but are in the Apocrypha of most Protestant Bibles—we read about the exploits of Judas Maccabeus who opposed the efforts of Antiochus Epiphanes (c. 166 B.C.E.) to suppress Jewish worship in Jerusalem (the contemporary Jewish festival of Hanukkah celebrates the successful revolt led by the Jews and their rededication of the Temple). In 4 Maccabees 18:7–8 a woman teaching her sons claims:

> I was a chaste maiden, and did not leave my father's house; but I kept guard over the rib built into woman's body. No seducer of the desert, nor deceiver in the field, corrupted me; nor did the seducing and beguiling Serpent defile my maidenly purity.[2]

The addition of her watching over "the rib that was built" is likely a reference to Eve's creation in Gen 2:22 and, in this instance, is related to the notion of her chastity and purity. The "corrupt beguiling Serpent" most likely refers to Satan, and it was from this enemy that she guarded her virginity. The sexual overtones of the passage leave little doubt that the author was referring to the tradition that the serpent had seduced Eve sexually in the garden.[3]

In the New Testament the most striking reference that may imply that Cain was born of Satan is 1 John 3:12. Since the epistle of 1 John highlights the theme of brotherly love, the figure of Cain, the murderer, provides the perfect antithesis to Christ. The author exhorts the believers not to be like Cain who was of the evil one and murdered his brother. And why did he murder him? Because his own deeds were evil and his brother's righteous. The question of Cain's origins arises from the phrase "who was of the evil one," which may be a reference to his satanic descent. Yet in v. 15 the author states in more general terms that "everyone who hates his brother is a murderer." It is interesting to note that the word for "murderer" is used only

1. b. Yeb. 103b. Cf. b. Shab. 146a; b. Abod. Zar. 22b.
2. Anderson, 4 Maccabees, 2:563.
3. Scarlata, Outside of Eden, 43–44.

here and in John 8:44, when Jesus calls the scribes and Pharisees children of the devil, who was a "murderer" from the beginning.

When we look at the dualistic nature of 1 John 3 as a whole we see the stark disparity the author creates between those who are "of God" and those who are "of the devil." In vv. 1–9 there is a sharp contrast between the "children of God," who no longer sin, and those "of the devil" who continue to sin. This argument is summed up in v. 10 where the author states, "By this it is evident who are the children of God, and who are the children of the devil: whoever does not practice righteousness is not of God, nor is the one who does not love his brother." The logic of the author naturally leads to Cain as the archetype of one who hates and kills his brother. And while there may be a possible allusion to Cain as the son of Satan, we need not conclude that 1 John 3 is speaking directly of Cain's satanic parentage here. Instead, the author declares that Cain was "of the evil one" because he committed murder and he did this because "his own deeds were evil and his brother's righteous" (v. 12). The rhetoric of 1 John contrasts those who love God and their brother with those who continue in sin (the word "brother" occurs fifteen times in 1 John alone). Cain, as the archetype of evil, is the perfect depiction of the human potential for hatred, envy, and murder. The use of this Old Testament character would have resonated with an audience familiar with the biblical story especially when considering Cain, the murderer, in contradistinction to Christ, the savior.

Why was Cain Evil and Abel Righteous?

Both Jewish and Christian interpreters seem to agree that Cain was wicked through-and-through and, of course, one can easily deduce this from the Genesis story. But there are other "evil" people in the Bible who get off slightly easier than Cain. So why does the elder brother come under such harsh criticism? Part of the answer probably lies in the nature of the literature that we are reading in Genesis 4. This portion of the Bible is often called the "Pre-history" or "Primeval History" (Genesis 1–11), which means the stories contained within might be interpreted typologically. In other words, the stories themselves become types that reflect all human behavior, rather than just that of the particular individual. Cain thus becomes the symbol of envy, rage, and murder, while Abel is cast as innocent and righteous despite the fact that we know nothing about him other than that he tended sheep and made an appropriate offering. Even Jesus makes a point of calling Abel, and his shed blood, "righteous" in Matt 23:35, when he speaks about the martyrdom of the prophets and others who have been rejected and killed. Yet even though Cain is portrayed as the archetype of evil in both Jewish and Christian traditions, they probably had different motivations behind their interpretations.

In the Jewish tradition there is often an effort to distance Cain from the descendants of Israel. One example comes from the rabbinic work *Pirkei de Rabbi Eliezer* (*PRE*) where it is written: "Rabbi Ishmael said: From Seth arose and were descended all the generations of the righteous, and from Cain arose and were descended all the generations of the wicked, who rebelled and sinned against Heaven." The delineation between the line of Seth and Cain was critical for the rabbis since it reinforced the depiction of Cain, and his offspring, as evil, and preserved a righteous lineage for Israel through Seth—this is all despite the fact that Cain's descendants were presumably wiped out by the flood in Genesis 6–8. Even Josephus, a first century (C.E.) Jewish historian, wrote of Cain's descendants:

> Thus, within Adam's lifetime, the descendants of Cain went to the depths of depravity, and, inheriting and imitating one another's vices, each ended worse than the last. They rushed incontinently into battle and plunged into brigandage; or if anyone was too timid for slaughter, he would display other forms of mad recklessness by insolence and greed. (*Ant.*, 1.66)

At least one motivation for Jewish interpreters in casting Cain as purely evil was to ensure that Israel's lineage did not stem from a murderous villain, but preserved its purity by coming through the line of Seth who was created in the likeness and image of his father, Adam (Gen 5:3).

When we turn to the early church fathers we find some of them still wrestling with the question of Cain's satanic origins, in spite of the clear stance of the Greek—or Latin—Bible that they would likely have read. Tertullian, writing on the benefits of patience, uses Cain's birth narrative as an example of what happened to the first couple after their remarkable display of impatience:

> For straightway [*sic*] that *impatience* conceived of the devil's seed, produced, in the fecundity of malice, anger as her [Eve's] son; and when brought forth, trained him in her own arts. For that very thing which had immersed Adam and Eve in death, taught their son, too, to begin with murder. (*Of Patience*, 5)

The allusion to Cain as the devil's seed is more prominent when he writes on the work of Christ:

> But (it will be said) Eve did not at the devil's word conceive in her womb. Well, she at all events conceived; for the devil's word afterwards became as seed to her that she should conceive as an outcast, and bring forth in sorrow. Indeed she gave birth to a fratricidal devil; whilst Mary, on the contrary, bare one who was one day to secure salvation to Israel . . . God therefore sent down into the virgin's womb His Word, as the good Brother, who should blot out the memory of the evil brother. (*On the Flesh of Christ*, 17)

Though Tertullian does not directly mention the sexual relationship between Eve and Satan, he compares the devil's word planted in Eve—which results in the birth of the "fratricidal devil"—with Mary's conceiving through "His Word" resulting in the birth of Jesus who overcame evil to bring salvation. Other church fathers make similar allusions to Cain's perverted origins, which demonstrate that the motif of Cain as the offspring of Satan was firmly identified with Gen 4:1 throughout generations of biblical interpreters.

For Christians, however, Cain's ruthless murder of his innocent brother also functioned as a foreshadowing of the Jews' rejection of Jesus and his crucifixion. In his work *Against Heresies*, Irenaeus, a late second-century bishop of Lyon, wrote on the appropriateness of offerings. In one section he compares the perfect offering of Christ to the impure offering of Cain who was "divided with envy and malice" in his heart. He goes on to cite the example of Christ's rebuking the Pharisees for their wickedness and hypocrisy and makes a direct comparison to Cain:

> For while they [the Pharisees] were thought to offer correctly so far as outward appearance went, they had in themselves jealousy like to Cain; therefore they slew the Just One, slighting the counsel of the Word, as did also Cain. (*Against Heresies*, 4.18.3)

With a clever interpretive twist, Irenaeus draws a direct connection between Cain's rejected offering and subsequent murder of Abel with the Pharisee's hypocritical offerings and their slaying of Christ. The result is that the entire Jewish race is now stained "with hands full of blood"[4] and they become a symbol of evil, hatred, and murder.

---

4. *Against Heresies*, 4.18.4.

In a similar interpretive move, Augustine, as we previously mentioned, describes Cain as the founder of the earthly city and treats the narrative in an allegorical manner. After providing a lengthy description of why Cain's sacrifice was rejected he writes:

> But Cain received that counsel of God in the spirit of one who did not wish to amend. In fact, the vice of envy grew stronger in him; and, having entrapped his brother, he slew him. Such was the founder of the earthly city. He was also a figure of the Jews who slew Christ the Shepherd of the flock of men, prefigured by Abel the shepherd of sheep: but as this is an allegorical and prophetical matter, I forbear to explain it now. (*City of God*, 15.7)

In this instance, Augustine uses Abel's occupation as a shepherd to link to Christ the "good shepherd" (John 10:11) and argues for the parallel between Cain and the Jews. Once again we see the church fathers interpreting the Old Testament typologically in the light of Jesus's life and ministry, but the outcome, in this particular instance, was extremely unfortunate and laid the foundations for a Christian polemic against the Jews that lasted throughout the Middle Ages and can still be felt today.

We could continue to list further examples of this type of interpretation, but the point is clear—for many early Christians the key to understanding certain Old Testament stories was to see them typologically, or as a foreshadowing of events that were fulfilled in the New Testament through the life of Christ and the newly formed church. While this type of analysis is by no means uncommon, and can often be appropriate in certain scriptural contexts, it can also be abused and can lead to the vilification of individuals or whole people groups. If we take the account of Genesis 4 as simply a moral tale of good and evil, then we too are liable to apply it to our contemporary context in a way that potentially excludes others from the grace of God and labels them as "evil." The difficulty with reducing any biblical text to some kind of lesson in morality is that we can fail to appreciate the emotional dynamics within the narrative and the complexity of what it means to grapple with the most profound issues that relate to our humanity.

Seeing Someone Face-to-Face

What is striking in the ancient translations and interpretations regarding Cain as either the son of Satan, or the embodiment of evil, is that, whatever the motivation, there seems to be a movement towards utter and complete exclusion. The notion that Cain descended from a fallen angel completely severs him not only from Adam, but also from the fellowship of all humanity. He is depicted as some sort of half-breed who shares satanic roots and is not even fit to be considered among the human race. Augustine portrays Cain as the founder of the earthly city and the incarnation of all that stands in antithesis to God and the heavenly city. Cain rises up against Abel out of jealousy, pride, and envy, and forsakes all relational interdependence with his brother to demonstrate his autonomy and power. By murdering Abel, Cain denies his sibling the right to live and treats him as Other. For many of the ancient interpreters Cain not only symbolizes the horrors of exclusion, but he himself becomes excluded from all who are "good" and is placed in the category of Other.

In his book *Exclusion and Embrace*, Miroslav Volf describes some of the characteristics of exclusion, which include being cut off from the bonds that connect us to one another. When people take themselves out of the pattern of interdependence, and place themselves in a position of sovereign independence, they exclude themselves from responsibility towards others. "The other then emerges either as an enemy that must be pushed away from the self and driven out of its space or as a nonentity—a superfluous being—that can be disregarded and abandoned."[5] It is this type of exclusion that is noticeably present in both Jewish and Christian portrayals of Cain. He is the enemy, the evil one, and should be forsaken and cast out to his inglorious end. Indeed, this is the way the Genesis narrative seems to conclude and we shall discuss later on whether the sign that God appoints for Cain was a mark of mercy or judgement.

For the moment, however, we can highlight the fact that interpreters throughout the ages have used Cain as a symbol of evil and have applied that label to others within their contemporary contexts in order to justify their own goodness or righteousness. Thus our retelling of the story can become a battle of "us" (Abel) versus "them" (Cain), rather than, as Westermann describes it, a story that reveals that every human being has the potential to be a murderer or to walk according to the ways of God.[6] While some modern commentators stress Gen 4:1–16 is a story of origins that relate to the tribe of the Kenites, the narrative should be read primarily as a story of two brothers; one who succumbs to envy, hatred, and murder, and the other who is victimized, dehumanized, and stripped of his life. We previously noted Augustine's view that the heavenly city and the earthly city

5. Volf, *Exclusion and Embrace*, 67.
6. Westermann, *Genesis 1–11*, 319.

exist side-by-side in this world, and in many ways, the desires of each city also reside in us (cf. Rom 7:15–25). So rather than approaching the figures of Cain and Abel as types for good and evil, and using them to label other individuals or groups, I suggest that we approach the humanity of each character as we come to grips with our own hatred and how we treat the Other.

When we consider our own capacity for the greatest good in relationships—or even the vilest evil—I appreciate the language used by French philosopher Emmanuel Levinas, when he speaks of coming "face-to-face" with the Other. He argues that in every social encounter, whether aggressive or benign, the Other stands in opposition to my own self. At the most basic level, this encounter need not be violent or hostile, but when standing face-to-face with another person they represent a threat to my unbridled desire or independence. Because of their presence, or their "face"—which, according to Levinas, is not just the literal face of someone, but represents a living being's inner thoughts, emotions, etc., present to another—I am forced to respond either in defence of my independence or in vulnerability—or "nudity" as Levinas might say—and dependence. The Other stands over and against myself but pleads for recognition, help, love, or even to share in a piece of broken bread. Fundamentally, I can respond to the person in one of two ways: I can desire their death or allow them to live. Now that might sound rather dramatic and certainly we (usually!) do not think about these things when first meeting someone. But the fact is, when we encounter the Other, we can either support their life in and through our relationship with them or we can let them die by our lack of response.

A simple example might help illustrate this point. If I come across an apple, a beautiful landscape or a rose bush in full bloom, I can choose to do with these things whatever I wish because they are *things*. But if I meet a person face-to-face, I must acknowledge their being, their right to exist and live, and hopefully they will do the same for me. Then, as a fellow human being, I am forced to make a decision: do I come to this person in vulnerability, seeking acceptance and risking their rejection? Or do I approach them with the desire to "kill" them by retaining my independence, by refusing my assistance, my help, or my love? Do I refuse to look them in the face, to see through the windows of their eyes, and reject their needs for the sake of my own domination? We can recall the actions of the priest and the Levite in the parable of the Good Samaritan, who, when they saw the man beaten and left for dead on the side of the road, passed by on the other side (Luke 10:29–37). What becomes particularly poignant in this story is the fact that the religious leaders "saw" the man, but refused to look at his face. They denied the victim his plea to live, to be helped and sustained, and, by avoiding all responsibility, they made the choice to "kill" rather than to give life. But the Samaritan approached the man, and, though it does not specifically say so in the passage, he looked on the man's face, into his eyes, and had compassion on him. He made the choice to give life rather than to take it away.

When we encounter the Other they make demands on our independence and dominion—"share with me," "make space for me," "help me," "sustain me," "heal me." To respond in violence is to disregard the face of another human being, to remain deaf to their pleas, and to refuse to look into their eyes. We essentially negate their existence and become murderers ourselves. Previously we looked at 1 John 3:12 and discussed the possibility that the author was alluding to Cain's satanic parentage when he wrote that he was "of the evil one," which would seem to cast the first murderer as one of "them" and not one of "us." Yet just before we can point the finger of condemnation at Cain, the author brings us back to the reality of our human condition and reminds us that, "everyone who hates his brother is a murderer" (1 John 3:15). No doubt this idea came from Jesus's preaching: "Whoever insults his brother will be liable to the council; and whoever says, 'You fool!' will be liable to the hell of fire" (Matt 5:22). For when we hate, we no longer see the face of the Other as one created in the image of God, but we regard them as nothing and avoid all responsibility towards them. In the language of 1 John, we can either choose to be "born of God" or "born of Satan" (vv. 9–10). Just as the (metaphorical?) seed of Satan was planted in Cain and brought forth hatred and murder from his heart, so too the believer in Christ can bring forth love because "the seed of God abides in him and he cannot keep on sinning because he has been born of God."

All of us—at one time or another—have chosen the path of Cain because we have allowed the seed of hatred to be sown in our own hearts and have refused to look on the face of the Other. This has resulted in our isolation from relationship and community. For most of us, this is far from being a one-time offense, but, instead, happens on a daily basis when we become angry with others, or refuse to give up our personal dominion and respond to the needs of others. We may not show an outward expression of hatred, but there is little difference when, at the moment we feel slighted, criticized, or attacked, we cut off another person from the gift of love that God wants us to share and we become cool, indifferent, or dispassionate.

EXCLUSION IN THE REST OF GENESIS

It is hatred that cuts us off from relationship and communion with one another and builds up walls that leave us in isolation, even from those closest to us. When we refuse to look upon someone's face we deny him or her the right to exist and to share in our fellowship. In Genesis the motif of exclusion, envy, and hatred begins with Cain and then weaves its way throughout the entire book and at each turn threatens to derail God's plan of salvation for the entire world. It begins with a promise to Abraham and it is worth reading this text once more since it serves as an interpretive key to Genesis and, indeed, for the whole of the Old Testament in God's calling and intention for Israel and all the families of the earth:

> Now the LORD said to Abram, "Go from your country and your kindred and your father's house to the land that I will show you. And I will make of you a great nation, and I will bless you and make your name great, so that you will be a blessing. I will bless those who bless you, and him who dishonors you I will curse, and in you all the families of the earth shall be blessed." (Gen 12:1–3)

Previously God had dealt with the whole world (Genesis 1–11), but now through the calling of a particular person, and through his descendants (i.e., the Israelites), he will use one family as the vehicle for his salvation. What may seem at first glance to be an emphatically exclusive relationship (and later covenant) with Abraham is, in fact, the path that will ultimately be a blessing to "all the families of the earth." Some find it difficult to accept the particularity of God's chosen people in the Old Testament and how that relates to the "openness" of Jesus in the New Testament offering salvation to both Jew and Gentile. But we can see from this passage in Genesis 12 that, from the beginning, God's plan for salvation has always included "all the families of the earth." Exclusivity was designed to achieve the greatest inclusivity, which is ultimately demonstrated in the life of Christ—the one and only beloved Son of the Father who would give his life for the salvation of the world (John 3:16). This design, however, is constantly on the brink of collapse throughout Genesis and the hostility and animosity between brothers—foreshadowed in Cain's murdering of Abel—provides a threat to God's intention of pouring out blessing upon all nations.

For God's promise to be fulfilled Abraham's family must grow, which meant that he must bear a son who must, in turn, produce more sons and daughters. In a sign of impatience with God's promise of an heir, Abraham's wife, Sarah, convinces him to sleep with their servant Hagar. The result is the birth of Ishmael but almost immediately Sarah, still barren and unable to produce a child, burns with anger toward Hagar and kicks her out of their home (Genesis 16). She can no longer stand to see her face. Under God's grace and direction, however, Hagar is brought back into their family, but by the time Sarah does give birth to Isaac, animosity rises to the surface again (Genesis 21) and Hagar and Ishmael are cast out permanently. Yet despite their being cut off from the chosen family, there is a remarkable act of grace demonstrated in the blessing God promises to Hagar that Ishmael will be made "into a great nation," which echoes the very promise God gave to Abraham in Genesis 12. As the promise of Abraham's blessing unfolds in the narrative of Isaac, the divisions and exclusion caused by envy and hatred place God's plan in jeopardy. And rather than familial harmony, the story of brotherly discord intensifies in the lives of Jacob and Esau.

From before their birth, we are told that Jacob and Esau were already battling within the womb (Gen 25:22–23). With such inauspicious beginnings we are only left to imagine what kind of struggles the brothers will face. Jacob—whose name is related to the Hebrew for "trickster" or "cheat"—convinces Esau to sell his birthright for a bowl of stew (Gen 25:27–34), which can hardly be seen as the most compassionate—or ethical—act since Esau was starving after having been out on the hunt. Later in the narrative Jacob deceives his father Isaac so that he will receive the firstborn's blessing and Esau is so infuriated that he makes a vow to himself: "I will kill my brother Jacob" (Gen 27:41). What remained unvocalized in the story of Cain and Abel now resonates in the words of Esau—when blessing is given to one and not the other, a murderous envy grows in the heart. Esau will no longer look into the eyes of Jacob—he has become Other. He denies Jacob his humanity and his right to live. Esau has fully justified fratricide in his own heart and knowing this, Jacob flees to Haran.

After some time, however, the brothers reunite (Genesis 32–33) and Jacob is terrified that Esau is still angry and is out for blood. Jacob sends messengers to his brother to try to diffuse the situation but when they finally meet, he bows down seven times before Esau. Yet rather than a knife through his heart, Jacob only feels the warmth of his brother's embrace and tears upon his neck as Esau weeps with joy. The wrestling of contention in the womb now comes full circle in the embrace of reconciliation. We do not know if Esau's wrath was appeased by Jacob's gifts, or his act of humility in prostrating himself upon the ground, but whatever the reason, Esau no longer regards Jacob as Other. He has realized that he is not a powerless victim and that the perpetrator, who so inflamed his rage, is not his enemy but is, as he calls him, "my brother" (Gen 33:9). Jacob, in response to such grace, says, "for truly to see your face is like seeing the face of God—since you have received me with such favor" (Gen 33:10). Both Jacob and Esau have seen each other face-to-face, in the fullest sense, and Jacob recognizes not only Esau's humanity, but the very reflection of God's glory in his brother's demonstration of mercy. In a dramatic conclusion to the narrative, forgiveness and reconciliation triumph over the endless cycle of vengeance and death. God's promise to Abraham will be fulfilled through Jacob and his twelve sons but not without one final scene where, once again, brotherly strife and envy over who should receive blessing comes to the forefront of the narrative.

The story of Joseph is by far the most dynamic and complex story in all of Genesis. The plot structure is unlike anything we have seen in the Genesis thus far, but the central motif of enmity between brothers provides the final link in a chain of events that began with Cain and Abel. Joseph is not unlike his father Jacob in that his character is far from perfect. He comes off like a tattletale in the beginning of the story when he brings a "bad report" to Jacob concerning his brothers (Gen 37:2). Joseph is already erecting walls and distancing himself from his siblings, but his father's favoritism and gift of a many-colored robe make matters worse. Once again fraternal antipathy grows to the point where his brothers hated him, "and cold not speak peaceably to him" (Gen 37:4). The bad situation quickly spirals out of control with Joseph's indiscreet revelation of his dreams and his brothers have had enough. He is no longer their sibling, but he has become Other and they cannot bear to look on his face. Indifferent to his fate, they violently expel him from their midst and cast him into a pit to leave him for dead.

The rest of the narrative follows Joseph's remarkable rise from prisoner to ruler over all of Egypt under Pharaoh. When famine hits the land, Joseph's brothers come to by food from him—though his identity is concealed—and he is confronted with the painful memories of his brutal separation from his family. After a series of "tests" (Gen 42:16), Joseph finally reveals himself through a wave a tears and the brothers are reconciled.

Jacob and his twelve sons are united once again. Murder, envy, and hatred have not won the day, but forgiveness and reconciliation usher in the hope that God's promise to Abraham will not be thwarted. The twelve tribes of Israel will descend to Egypt (Genesis 46–50) and the promise of offspring, blessing and becoming a great nation will continue to be unveiled throughout Exodus and the rest of the Old Testament.

From the murder of Abel to the reconciliation of Joseph and his brothers, the author of Genesis masterfully depicts the workings of the human heart in community and the potential that we all have to either exclude or embrace. The characters of Cain, Esau, and Joseph's brothers all reflect the capacity we possess to reject the moral and ethical demands that come with seeing another human being face-to-face. They act as victims of their own circumstances. They detach themselves from their perceived perpetrator and consider their brother as their enemy. Thankfully, however, this is not the end of the story because we also witness the ability to put aside hatred and envy to embrace forgiveness and to extend hospitality and reconciliation. We see the restoration of community and the bond of love reestablished between Jacob and Esau, and Joseph and his brothers, which begins to fill out God's promise to Abraham.

The story of Cain and Abel, as well as the rest of Genesis, is not black and white. It depicts the realities of life where people often fail and no one is perfect. Yet through it all there is a divine plan that keeps pressing forward. It is God's mission to bless all the families of the earth, but its fullness will only be revealed when God's people live according to his love. Though God's promise was fulfilled on various levels throughout the Old Testament, its fullest expression would not be complete until the coming of his Son and is now further being fulfilled through the work of the church.

Standing on the other side of the death and resurrection of Jesus, it is apparent why the author of 1 John so passionately condemns hatred and murder. He has seen the history of what it can do to humanity, and especially God's people, but now he proclaims a new way—not the way of Cain, but the way of Christ and the way of sacrificial love. This love is an unending invitation to join in the fellowship of the Father, the Son, and the Holy Spirit, and to be in union with one another in the living body of Christ, the church. It is an invitation to see one another face-to-face with veils torn off and clothed with the vulnerability, humility, and love of Christ. Yet how do we convey such a love in a globalized society that is increasingly dominated by Internet technologies where communication lacks a physical presence and frequently takes place without seeing someone face-to-face?

HOSPITALITY AND BREAKING BREAD IN THE VIRTUAL WORLD

In an age where global communication can actually lead to further disconnect and disassociation, citizens of the heavenly city can seek out new ways to extend the gift of healing and the embrace of Christ whether in their local surroundings or in the virtual world. And if death of the Other comes through our inability, or refusal, to see our neighbor face-to-face, then the redemption of such exclusion comes through hospitality, which is the invitation to come into community, to share in fellowship, and to break bread in communion with one another. The mark of Christian citizens in the twenty-first century is that they no longer recognize the exclusion of anyone, but, instead, they open their doors in hospitality to the poor and to those in need of restoration whether it be a physical door or a virtual door.

The word "hospitality" comes from the Latin root *hospes*, which means a host, or someone who invites in, and takes care of, strangers or visitors. In the Old Testament hospitality is expressed in a variety of ways, but perhaps the most striking commandment is God's imperative to show compassion to the fatherless, the widow, and the sojourner (e.g., Exod 22:22; Deut 10:18; 14:29; 24:20–21; 26:12; Ps 146:9). Our responsibility to care for others is to extend beyond the inner circles of our family and friends to those on the periphery of society. This commandment required the community of Israel, as part of its covenant obedience, to protect those who were defenseless and were the most at risk of being abused or oppressed. The commandment, however, was not simply about extending charity to those in need, but, rather, it was about providing justice to those who are vulnerable, or incapable of defending themselves, and creating a safe space for them to grow and thrive.

To practice hospitality means that we invite others in to become a part of our family or community and, in doing so, they too can become givers into the common life. Hospitality is not merely generosity towards the poor, but, rather, it is founded on a communality that recognizes each person's worth and unique contribution to the whole despite whether they have or have not. When a person is welcomed into a place where anxiety, insecurity, and violence cease they can let down their defenses and begin to share and grow in the gifts that God has given them. When we offer hospitality we begin to see others face-to-face and recognize that they too bear the image of God. And when we begin to see God's image in others we recognize not only their needs, but also our own and how our life together requires both giving and receiving.

Archbishop Desmond Tutu was instrumental in bringing about forgiveness and reconciliation in South Africa after years of brutality and suffering under apartheid. Though retribution and revenge would have been expected after decades of oppression, he points out why the way of amnesty was consistent with African thinking and the notion of *ubuntu*. He describes *ubuntu* as being generous, hospitable, caring, and compassionate based on the understanding that each person is inextricably bound up with other people ("A person is a person through other persons"). He goes on to say:

> A person with ubuntu is open and available to others, affirming of others, does not feel threatened that others are able and good, for he or she has a proper self-assurance that comes from knowing that he or she belongs in a greater whole and is diminished when others are humiliated or diminished, when others are tortured or oppressed, or treated as if they were less than who they are.[7]

Sometimes I find that simply using a word from another language is helpful in filling out what we mean by certain words in English. The term *ubuntu* reminds me that an important part of our understanding—and practice—of hospitality is a proper self-assurance in our own identity as beloved children of God, created and renewed in his image. The more firmly we are rooted in that knowledge and experience the more we will be able to demonstrate the type of hospitality that can give life to others, even in the most tragic of circumstances like the devastation experienced in South Africa because of apartheid. So whether you prefer the term *ubuntu* or not, how do we become people who practice hospitality in an age where communication no longer requires our physical presence or seeing someone face-to-face? How do citizens of the heavenly city demonstrate hospitality in such a way as to make people feel part of a (virtual) community being loved, welcomed, and feeling a sense of belonging?

I must admit that I have been skeptical of the notion of Internet-based "communities" since there is a loss of physical presence that is critical to our interaction with one another. My tendency was to dismiss them altogether

---

7. Tutu, *No Future without Forgiveness*, 34–35.

but after speaking with Brian Hardin, who runs a podcast called the Daily Audio Bible (www.dailyaudiobible.com), which now has over a million subscribers, I was forced to adjust my thinking. Brian began by broadcasting a Scripture reading followed by a thought for the day and, in his relaxed, conversational style, Brian's wisdom and insights have encouraged (literally) millions of people. He began with the desire to share the Bible with others and the Internet provided the perfect medium to reach people all around the world.

Brian did not produce the Daily Audio Bible with the intention of creating a global community, but soon after he began in 2006 he started receiving hundreds of emails a day from people all over the world who wanted to connect with him and share their stories. It was one email, however, that had a profound impact on Brian and he began to realize how powerful the Internet can be in extending hospitality through God's word. The email came from a young woman at university who was struggling in her life and was battling anorexia. She had become so distressed that she physically could not leave her house until one day when she found the Daily Audio Bible website and listened to the Scriptures for eight hours straight. She soon gave her life to Christ and encouraged Brian to set up some sort of forum where people listening to the Scriptures could also connect with one another. Soon after that chat rooms, social networking, and phone lines opened up for people all over the world who shared one thing in common—a love for the Bible. A community was created out of people coming to Scripture for nourishment. And this is a point that Brian emphasizes, since the Daily Audio Bible is unabashedly about the centrality of Scripture and that the online community is never centered around a particular individual.

In the beginning Brian regarded the Internet as a thing—something we use as a tool to do whatever it is that we are trying to accomplish. But over time, he began to regard the Internet as a place—a place where people could come in anonymity or full disclosure and interact with other people. The Internet offers its own setting where social relations are being lifted out of their local contexts and are being restructured in a world where time and space no longer matter. People from all over the globe can make use of the Daily Audio Bible's resources, chat rooms, prayer rooms, international missions, kids programs, and forums and, in the process, create and sustain a virtual community. At any time people can join in conversations and retain a level of anonymity if desired, which can be important for those who might have had hurtful experiences with the church or other communities in the past. Participants can pray for others in different countries around the world and have direct knowledge of what is happening to those whom they are praying for.

Another significant resource that online communities can offer is a place for confession. Like the traditional anonymity associated with confession to a priest in the Catholic Church, people are invited to share their struggles and confess things that have been a burden in their lives. In some Christian communities there are often taboo sins that remain unspoken inside the walls of the church—things like Internet pornography addiction, adultery, or other vices that people find difficult to share without feeling like they will be judged. In these instances, people can confess in an online group—or to Brian, who is an Anglican priest—and begin the healing process. Virtual communities, therefore, offer a meeting place for those from any part of the globe, at any time of day, to come and connect to others in a meaningful way. We previously spoke of hospitality as inviting in the stranger, the sojourner, and the Other to care for them and provide for their needs while also creating a space for them to heal and grow so that they too might contribute to the community. And this is exactly what virtual communities can do in ways that physical communities cannot. Virtual communities can exist for all people—connected to the Internet—at all times and are not bound by things like bad weather, poor health, or the person who forgets to bring the keys to open the church!

Brian is aware, however, of the walls that are created by being in a virtual community. Some of them are obviously insurmountable—like being physically present—but this has not stopped him, or those who are a part of the Daily Audio Bible community, from doing everything possible to connect people. In an effort to somehow localize the community that was developing on the Internet, Brian launched the Windfarm Café, where he and others initially met as a church and then later opened up as a café during the week. In his experience he has found that many people will not go into a church, but might come to a café as a neutral zone. They offer weekly worship services that are broadcast on the Internet and shared by people around the world. For Brian, the Windfarm Café represents the vision that communities still need to reach out to the people who are physically around them and his hope is that their Internet presence stimulates "real" gatherings around the world where people can meet and grow together.

One potential danger of virtual communities is the possibility of promoting an unhealthy pattern of detachment from physical social engagement. Many people today are more comfortable staring into a monitor than they are interacting with another human being face-to-face, which we shall discuss further in chapter 6. While there will always be the tension of trying to find bridges between virtual reality and the real world, this does not mean the two cannot coexist. Though there is always the underlying hope that people will connect to one another in the physical presence of a gathered community, for some this may not be a possibility. A virtual gathering might be the only "real" community a person can experience, and in such instances the church now has the opportunity to provide such a place.

For Christians today the use of the Internet—and other information technologies—can be critical in extending hospitality to those longing to be in community and in connecting them to an initial experience of love and belonging. Whether this is done through chat groups, social networking, or websites, we can enter these (virtual) places and be a significant presence there. This is not to say that every church must have its own online community or chat room, but we can connect to communities that already exist or form new ones based on geographical location, interests, or whatever might draw people together. The point is to begin offering bridges to those in need of hospitality by using the tools that are unique to this generation. Centuries of Christians have never had the opportunity to pray in an online chat room, or care for someone who lives thousands of miles away, or confess their sins anonymously online, but now that opportunity exists and it would be a shame to squander it.

I do not think, however, that the issues regarding virtual communities and physical communities require an either/or answer. The purpose of hospitality is a globalized society is not to substitute online communities with real ones, but, rather, to allow them both to live fluidly in a symbiotic relationship whereby one might feed into another. Both types of communities are needed and while the virtual world offers new ways to think about how we extend hospitality and participate in the community of Christ, we are still responsible for those people who surround us (physically) on a daily basis. Looking back again to 1 John 3 we are challenged by the simplicity of what it means to care for someone else: "But if anyone has the world's goods and sees his brother in need, yet closes his heart against him, how does God's love abide in him? Little children, let us not love in word or talk but in deed and in truth" (vv. 17–18). The author reminds us that no matter how much we talk about loving others we cannot forget that it requires action on our part—whether that is praying for someone online or physically giving to a person in need. In either case, Christians today have the opportunity to do both where faith is something to be acted out in the physical and virtual world.

The danger we face today, however, is that we can fail to love in "deed and truth" if we use the convenience of Internet technologies as a substitute for the work it requires to sustain healthy relationships. Is it enough to respond to someone via email when I should really call them or meet with them face-to-face? Is it enough to post a response on Twitter when I should invite a person out for coffee to discuss the matter? Is it enough to "friend" someone on Facebook when I should have the person over to my house for dinner? Do I feel satisfied with my contribution to society because I clicked the Facebook "like" button on someone's disaster relief website? Since social networking and other mediums have the potential to devalue relationships, it is up to us to determine when we are being authentic with others and loving in "deed and truth" and when we are using technologies only to love in "word or talk."

Living as a Christian citizen in a world of Internet technologies and social networking presents all sorts of questions about how we might live faithfully and show hospitality to those in need. Yet despite technological advancements, we are still surrounded by brokenness, isolation, and exclusion that destroy relationships and community. In the ancient Jewish and Christian interpretation of Cain's birth we saw the tendency to cast Cain as Other—born of Satan and a symbol all that is evil. Rather than seeing his humanity, many interpreters chose to highlight his perverted birth in the light of his murderous actions. Designating someone as Other not only occurs in biblical interpretation but continues today when we choose not to look at someone face-to-face, when we ignore their plea for life, and when we disregard their humanity and intrinsic worth as a child of God. Whether we are confronted by an Islamic extremist, a devout atheist, or a poor person on the street, it is through hospitality that we acknowledge a person's value and create a space where their needs can be met, where they can grow and begin to give back into the lives of others. This might take place in the real world, or in a virtual world, but wherever it is, hospitality is an authentic expression of love that mirrors the invitation of the Father through the Son and through the Holy Spirit. God's initiative in Jesus's life, death, and resurrection has already created a space for all humanity to grow, and now the church has the opportunity to extend that invitation in both physical and virtual reality.

3 Worship and Consumerism

Offering Our Best

In the course of time Cain brought to the LORD an offering of the fruit of the ground, and Abel also brought of the firstborn of his flock and of their fat portions. And the LORD had regard for Abel and his offering, but for Cain and his offering he had no regard. So Cain was very angry, and his face fell.

—GENESIS 4:3–5

A FRIEND TOLD ME a true story about a woman who went into a jewelry store looking to purchase a silver cross as a gift. While she was browsing the display case a worker came over to help her find one that would be suitable. The saleswoman scanned over the different crosses and then blithely asked, "Would you like one with a man on it or without a man?" I have to admit that I had quite a laugh at the fact that someone would ask such a question, but it was a poignant reminder that we are living in a post-Christian, Western consumer culture. We are no longer surrounded by those who are familiar with the biblical narratives, or by those who once filled the church's pews out of a sense of duty or obligation. Instead, we are confronted with the sovereignty of individual customers who, in many cases, will have little to do with church or, if they do, might pick and choose their place of worship like they do the latest article of clothing. This is not to say that our culture is either better or worse than previous generations, but, instead, it offers us a new reality in which the church must find its voice.

In the previous chapter we considered the opportunity Christian citizens have to extend hospitality to those who are present in both the physical and virtual world. In the following discussion we shall explore the foundations of the globalized society in the West and the rise of consumerism and what affect this might have on worship.

Though it is often thought that consumerism is equivalent to excessive materialism, we shall see that there are deeper issues of identity and fulfillment that underlie a lifestyle based on the consumption of goods and services. If Augustine had been writing today, he might have been tempted to call the "earthly city" the "consumer city" since commoditization and consumption have become so central to Western culture. And when we look at citizens of today's consumer city, we find that they are driven by an endless search for self-expression and self-discovery, which desperately tries to satisfy spiritual longings with material things. Yet no matter how voracious one's consumption is, the emptiness remains. In contrast, however, to the individualistic, self-serving pursuit of consumerism we are offered an alternative way of life in the heavenly city—a life of worship. Worship, as we shall see in Cain and Abel and the rest of the Old Testament, is a grateful response to God that is marked by the faith of the worshiper as well as the material gift, which represents a sacrifice of the greatest value. Citizens of God's kingdom learn to surrender what is most precious in the world's eyes so that they might find their true identity in relationship with the living God. And rather than the self-obsessed isolation of consumerism, worship invites us into a community of believers—the body of Christ—where we discover who we are amidst the communion of saints.

Turning back to our story of the two brothers, we come to the first act of worship recorded in the Bible. And though we do not have the weight of consumerism bearing down on the biblical narrative, we discover what is at the heart of true and acceptable worship in God's eyes. We are not told why Cain and Abel bring their sacrifices to the Lord, and, indeed, we know nothing of how they understood what a sacrifice was in the first place. But the author is not concerned with these details and we get the sense, right from the start, that they both had some knowledge of what they were doing and why they were doing it. There is something in the act of worship— no matter what religion—that requires sacrifice and offering. We give up something to God out of gratitude for all that he has given us. It is an act that stands squarely in the face of consumerism and remains in conflict with the very fabric of our modern society.

It would not be an exaggeration to say that, in the last two centuries, consumerism has been a massive force in shaping how we live and how we form our identities. In the light of such changes, we might ask how the first act of worship speaks to the twenty-first-century Christian who is daily immersed in a society fueled by marketing and consumption. How do citizens of the heavenly city bring their best offering in worship and how does that stand in opposition to the consumer city in which we live?

Interpreters over the centuries have debated why God rejected Cain's offering but accepted Abel's. At first glance it seems that there is no reason for God's rejection of Cain and his offering. Is this a sign of God's capriciousness? Does he accept some and not others simply because he chooses to do so? Some scholars contend that the story is about the conflict between shepherds and farmers in the early history of Israel and that, since the pastoral life was more pleasing to God, animal offerings were superior to vegetable offerings, or that animal sacrifice was better because it contained blood. What is most problematic about this theory is that it is nowhere apparent in the earlier—or later—chapters of Genesis that the agrarian life is inferior to the pastoral life. In fact, five chapters later we are told that Noah became a "man of the soil" (Gen 9:20) and planted a vineyard. We may also note that throughout the rest of the Old Testament farming is central to the life of the Israelites, and so there must be some other reason for God's rejection of Cain's "fruits of the earth."

Others argue that the key to understanding God's rejection can be found in the lengthy description of Abel's offering as being "of the first born of his flock and of their fat portions," which essentially means that he offered from the very best of what he had. Cain, on the other hand, brought only "from the fruits of the earth." The description is less specified and what is noticeably absent is the term "first fruits," which is often used throughout the Old Testament to depict the best of the crops that were offered to God on various occasions. By leaving out a more detailed account of Cain's offering, it appears that the author is stressing the superior quality of Abel's sacrifice. While the narrative does not explicitly condemn Cain for bringing a second-rate gift, it does seem to lean in that direction.

Another rhetorical device that potentially helps us understand God's response is how the author draws our attention to the fact that God looked upon, or "had regard for," Abel *and* his offering, but did not have regard for Cain *and* his offering. The seemingly minor inclusion of God looking not just on the sacrifices but on the brothers themselves appears to highlight God's attention to the inner attitude of the worshiper in conjunction with the content of his gifts. Though the story does not spell this out, we might assume that Abel approached God with a humble heart, and with fear and reverence, which is demonstrated by his choice offerings. Cain, on the other hand, exemplifies the one who offers, but does so merely out of obligation, with contempt in his heart. Again, the narrative does not spell this out for us but the subtle inclusions and exclusions in the text might lead us to think that truly acceptable worship is both a matter of what we offer—in terms of physical material—and how we offer it—in terms of our heart and faith. The story, however, still remains somewhat ambiguous and open to different interpretations, which is what we find in the ancient commentators.

The LXX version provides some differentiation between the brothers' offerings by translating the same Hebrew word with different Greek words. While the Hebrew word for "offering" is the same in vv. 3–5, the translator uses "gift" to describe what Abel brings to God. So the translation in English would read:

> And it came about after some days that Cain brought to the Lord an *offering* of the fruits of the earth and Abel, he also brought of the firstlings of his sheep and of their fat portions. And God looked upon Abel and upon his *gifts*, but to Cain and to his *offerings* he did not pay attention.

While "gifts" and "offerings" might have been heard differently by a Greek audience, the use of two different words makes it seem like there was a contrast between what Abel offered and what Cain offered.

In the Latin translation Jerome slightly embellishes his rendering of v. 3 with "after *many* days," whereas the Hebrew would normally be translated more generally as "After some time . . ." or "It came about . . ." Jerome may have been influenced by Philo's commentary on Cain in which he argues that the elder brother delayed bringing his sacrifice while Abel brought his offering without hesitation.[1] The emphasis here is not on the actual material of Cain's offering, but the spirit in which he offers it. Cain's delay is a sign of his reluctance to bring a sacrifice to God and, since he is unwilling to bring something out of a grateful and thankful heart, he is rejected.

Ephrem the Syrian argues that Cain did not make a wise choice in his offering, but brought only "young grains," rather than from the bulls or calves that he possessed. He writes, "But because Cain had taken such little regard for the first offering that he offered, God refused to accept it in order to teach Cain how he was to make an offering." For Ephrem, Cain's

---

1. *Sacrifices*, 52; QG 1:60.

inability to bring his best to God demonstrated that he had "no love for the One who would receive his offering." He concludes, "Abel's offering was accepted, therefore, because of his discrimination, whereas that of Cain was despised because of his negligence." Many of the ancient rabbinic interpretations share similar criticisms and contend that Cain brought from his inferior crops (*Gen. Rab.* 22.5), or that he offered the "remnants of his meal of roasted grain, the seed of flax" (*PRE* 21). In all these interpretations the deficiency of the physical offering is seen as a reflection of the heart of the worshiper. Since Cain was reluctant to part with the best material things that he had, he demonstrated his lack of faith and gratefulness to the God who provided them in the first place.

Tg. Ps.-J., however, takes a decidedly different interpretation of Cain's rejection by locating the offering at the time of Passover. It translates:

> And it was after some time, on the fourteenth of Nisan, that Cain brought from the fruit of the earth, from the seed of flax, an offering of first fruits before the Lord. And Abel, he also brought from the firstborn of the flock and from their fat ones, and there was pleasure before the Lord and he showed favor to Abel and to his offering. But to Cain and to his offering he did not show favor, and Cain was very angry and the expression of his face was downcast.

There was a tendency in ancient Judaism to associate significant events with the month of Nisan because of its importance in the Jewish calendar. Yet by placing the offering at the time of Passover, Tg. Ps.-J. subtly imposes the Mosaic laws regarding the prescribed sacrifices on the narrative (Exod 12:3–6; Lev 23:10–14). Abel's offering of his firstborn sheep fits perfectly within Passover requirements, but Cain's offering of flax seed would have been completely inappropriate. Despite the anachronism—Moses's law coming centuries after Cain and Abel—the Targum portrays Abel as a foreshadowing of what true Israelite worship and sacrifice should be. What is of interest is that Tg. Ps.-J. speaks of Cain's offering as a "gift of first fruits," and is, to my knowledge, the only interpretation to say explicitly that Cain brought his best. For Tg. Ps.-J. Cain's sin is not so much about bringing a gift of inferior quality, but has to do with a cultic offense that neglected the requirements of the Passover sacrifice.

Augustine, however, argued that Cain did not rightly "distinguish" his offering and did not bring what was worthy of the one true God. Instead, he brought a gift not out of gratitude but in hopes of gaining something that would satisfy his evil desires. Augustine sees Cain's failed offering as a sign of the earthly city and its desire to seek God only in hopes of getting something in return. Rather than loving good for the sake of peace and the well-being of the community, citizens of the earthly city offer to the gods to satisfy themselves and that they might rule over their enemies. "The good use the world that they may enjoy God: the wicked, on the contrary, that they may enjoy the world would fain use God."[2] While making offerings to the gods for one's benefit is not a common practice in most Western societies—though it is common in other countries throughout the world—contemporary parallels still exist in the church today among those who might give mediocre offerings of their time or resources in expectation of fantastic blessings from God in return. They might think of God like a vending machine—if they put just enough in (e.g., prayers, service, or offerings) they will get what they want in return. Citizens of God's kingdom, however, offer out of blessing and thanksgiving, expecting nothing in return (Luke 6:35).

In looking at this first act of worship it is easy to see why the ancient interpreters placed the blame on Cain for his inability to bring an appropriate offering rather than focusing on God's potential capriciousness. Cain might have been rejected because of his tardiness, or the poor quality of his gift, or even for breaking Passover regulations. But whatever the reason for his rejection, all the interpreters touch on one of the central issues regarding worship in the Bible—how does what we offer in worship relate to what we believe and how we live? Do the physical gifts we bring have some correspondence to our faith and obedience to God's commandments? The answer is, as we shall see, that the act of worship requires both the material and the spiritual and that the two are inseparable when we bring our offerings before the Lord.

Worship and Sacrifice in the Old Testament

Later on in Israel's history, the prophet Amos was one of the prominent voices to address this issue. During a time of excessive material wealth and military success the Israelites of Amos's day continued to bring the prescribed offerings to the temple, but their lives stood in stark contrast to the justice, love, and mercy God wanted them to display. They trampled on the poor, demonstrated a blatant disregard for justice, and mistreated the vulnerable in society that they were charged to protect. In words that drip with sarcasm, God responds to their abuses:

2. St. Augustine, *City of God*, 15.7.

> "Come to Bethel, and transgress;
>   to Gilgal, and multiply transgression;
> bring your sacrifices every morning,
>   your tithes every three days;
> offer a sacrifice of thanksgiving of that which is leavened,
>   and proclaim freewill offerings, publish them;
> for so you love to do, O people of Israel!"
>   declares the Lord GOD. (Amos 4:4–5)

The Israelites had completely divorced the material offering from faith and the ethical life that they were called to live under the Law. In doing so, they imagined that their covenant relationship with God would be fine as long as they followed the rules, gave from their material possessions, and worshiped according to the correct procedures. Yet what was God's response to this type of disconnect in worship?

> I hate, I despise your feasts,
>   and I take no delight in your solemn assemblies.
> Even though you offer me your burnt offerings and grain offerings,
>   I will not accept them;
> and the peace offerings of your fattened animals,
>   I will not look upon them.
> Take away from me the noise of your songs;
>   to the melody of your harps I will not listen.
> But let justice roll down like waters,
>   and righteousness like an ever-flowing stream.
> (Amos 5:21–24)

The poetic brilliance of Amos's condemnation makes it all the more powerful. God cannot bear to listen to the shrill of worship music that is accompanied by corruption and exploitation, but, rather, he longs to hear the thunderous roar of rushing waters that resound when his people establish justice on the earth. We cannot think of much stronger language than "hate" or "despise" when it comes to what the Lord thinks of our worship, but the message is loud and clear—true worship requires our offerings to be accompanied by faith, which manifests itself in the daily expression of love, justice, and mercy. Without these, our gifts are worthless in God's eyes.

Psalm 51 is another example of the tension between worshiping the Lord with a faithful heart and yet offering the appropriate material gifts. The psalmist initially seems to dismiss the importance of a physical sacrifice when he writes:

> For you will not delight in sacrifice, or I would give it;
> > you will not be pleased with a burnt offering.
> The sacrifices of God are a broken spirit;
> > a broken and contrite heart, O God, you will not despise. (Ps 51:16–17)

For those who might want to emphasize the spiritual aspect of worship, this passage seems to justify the notion that God is not concerned with what we physically offer, but, rather, is only concerned about our hearts. While some scholars contend that vv. 18–19 are a later addition to the psalm, this deeply inward, spiritual confession ends with God delighting in the prescribed temple offerings:

> Then will you delight in right sacrifices,
> > in burnt offerings and whole burnt offerings;
> then bulls will be offered on your altar. (Ps 51:19)

In other words, God will not take pleasure in material offerings that are brought without a "broken and contrite heart," but he *will* take pleasure in the material gift when it is offered in faith. Rather than being an addition to the text, it seems that these final verses accurately sum up the balance between the material and spiritual components of worship.

In the New Testament we find the striking example of Ananias and Sapphira, who are a part of the first community of believers in Jerusalem after Pentecost. Like other faithful members, they sold a piece of land and offered the proceeds to the apostles to be distributed among any who had need (Acts 5:1–10). But rather than offering the full amount, they kept some back and, presumably, lied to Peter about the offering they gave. In a stern rebuke Peter tells them they had the choice to offer freely whatever they wanted. But because they tried to deceive others—and God—they both fell dead at the apostles' feet. The dramatic conclusion to this short story in Acts serves as poignant reminder of the connection that exists between the attitude of one's heart and the offerings one presents to God.

So was Cain rejected because of his inadequate offering, or was it because of his lack of faith? I believe that it was probably both, and that an inferior, or unacceptable, offering was an outward reflection of his unbelief. The author of the letter to the Hebrews seems to make this very point when he writes:

> By faith Abel offered to God a more acceptable sacrifice than
> Cain, through which he was commended as righteous, God

49

commending him by accepting his gifts. And through his faith,
though he died, he still speaks. (Heb 11:4)

The author begins the chapter by defining faith as "the assurance of things
hoped for, the conviction of things not seen." Abel was so convinced of the
holiness and power of the living God that he brought a sacrifice that was
of the greatest value. He saw beyond the economic worth of his firstborn
sheep—which would have been extremely valuable—because it paled in
comparison to the profound gift of life given by the Creator. Seeing his
faith, God commended him as righteous and accepted what he had offered.
The reverse seems to be true of Cain—he did not share the same faith and
assurance as Abel, and, as a result, brought an unacceptable sacrifice.

CONSUMERISM AND THE SEARCH FOR IDENTITY

One of the responsibilities of citizens of the heavenly city is to share the
story of God's love and offer of salvation through Christ in a relevant way
that engages with people in any time or place. And if we are to share the
gospel in a globalized society dominated by consumerism, then we first
need to understand the patterns and values of that culture. In his classic
text, *Christ and Culture*, H. R. Niebuhr reminds us that human beings do
not come to Christ without approaching him through their own cultural
lens:

> Christ claims no man as a purely natural being, but always as one
> who has become human in culture; who is not only in culture, but
> into whom culture has penetrated. Man not only speaks but thinks
> with the aid of the language of culture. Not only has the objective
> world about him been modified by human achievement; but the
> forms and attitudes of his mind which allow him to make sense
> out of the objective world has been given him by culture.[3]

If, then, we are immersed in a consumer culture, how can Christians be
a relevant witness of the gospel and remain true to its basic truths? Do
we have to become anti-consumerists in order to set an example of what
it means to live a Christ-like life in the world? Personally, I do not think
that we need to abandon our culture, or remove ourselves from the market
economy, in order to live faithfully as citizens of God's kingdom. I do, however, believe that it is helpful to take a step back from our culture so that

---

3. Niebuhr, *Christ and Culture*, 69.

we might examine it from a different perspective. For today's Christian this requires pausing to reflect thoughtfully on what it means to live daily in an environment that is saturated with advertising, marketing, and the beliefs and values of a consumer society. Though we belong to the heavenly city, we still live and breathe in the air of the consumer city and so—for the sake of perspective—we must make our way to the mountaintops every so often to get a clear view of what lies below.

Most of us recognize the rampant materialism of our culture and often associate consumerism with greed and the inordinate desire to gain material things. While this represents one aspect of consumerism, it is only the tip of the iceberg. When we sink deep below the surface we discover not only materialism, but also an endless quest for fulfilment and the longing to discover who we really are. Every human being is searching for his or her personal identity and for what will ultimately fulfill his or her desires. This condition of the human soul is articulated by Augustine, who, at the beginning of his *Confessions*, writes, "You have made us for yourselves, and our heart is restless until it finds its rest in you."[4] Augustine knew that at the core of every human being is the longing to know and to be known—to know who we are, and to be known by the one who created us. The restlessness of the human heart compels us to find fulfillment and to enter into the rest that can only come from God. Yet so often we seek other means to fulfillment, which ultimately end in emptiness and a continued struggle to find what will give us satisfaction.

In previous generations men and women have pursed philosophy, the arts, political power, or one's vocation, in order to fill that infinite void. In today's world, however, the average person is conditioned to believe that who we are, and what we are, is determined by what we consume. In other words, we are taught—subliminally in many instances—that our identity is indistinguishable from the goods and services we consume. Whether it is the house, the car, the clothes, the food we buy, the vacations we take, the restaurants we eat at, or the films we see—in a consumer society, all of these things contribute to one's identity. If we want to be beautiful, the advertisements tell us that we must use this makeup or that skin cream. If we want to feel successful, we are told that we must drive this type of car or own that type of kitchen. If we want to feel confident, we must wear this clothing or start that diet or the latest exercise fad. In all of these things we are given the message that if we consume X, then we will become Y. So how did we get to this place in history?

4. St. Augustine, *Confessions*, 3.

In the nineteenth and twentieth centuries there was an artistic movement called Romanticism that is often identified with poets such as Wordsworth, Shelley, or Coleridge and painters like the Pre-Raphaelites. Romanticism emphasized the uniqueness of an individual's personality and the infinite capacity each person has as a creative artist. For the Romantics, true art was an expression of this interior feeling of infiniteness. They believed that life was experienced through self-expression, self-discovery, and the pursuit of pleasure. Peter Sedgwick argues that today's consumerism is the product of a romantic belief based on infinite desire in the quest for finding the self.[5] This Romantic fascination with the individual soul is reflected in the modern consumer. Yet rather than seeking our identity through artistic expression and creativity, like the Romantics, the consumer is focused primarily on pleasure, self-expression, and individual discovery through consumption. In a world where faith has been abandoned people must find the means through which they might discover their identity, and one vehicle for self-discovery has become mass consumption. Sedgwick goes on to say that "consumerism is a displaced search for identity, from the religious vocation found in work in previous centuries to a combination of hedonism and self-expression in consumption."[6] Products are, therefore, not just purchased, or consumed, to fulfill our desires—they define who we are.

Consumerism is one of the most significant phenomena of our modern society that shapes how we identify and imagine ourselves to be. Consumption is about feeling, style, and desire, where personal choice is equivalent to freedom. The sovereignty of the individual is paramount and individuals exerts their "freedom" by choosing what they will consume (consequently, if people do not have purchasing power, or the means to consume, they can be excluded from mainstream society and feel as though their freedom has been restricted). One finds fulfillment in the act of choosing for their own pleasure, and meaning in the act of self-gratification. With the elevation of consumer autonomy, the marketing world perpetually feeds us the story that if we only have *this* product, or if we only go on *this* holiday, or eat at *this* restaurant, our lives will be fulfilled.

I recall a car commercial that showed a man walking out into a nearly empty parking garage late at night while the voiceover said something like, "You've worked hard. . . you deserve it." And the man opened the door of

5. Sedgwick, *The Market Economy and Christian Ethics*, ch. 2.

6. Ibid., 136.

his luxury vehicle and drove off. The message is clear—if you give up the majority of your life to make money, then you should have the freedom to choose what to do with your money. And if you are successful, you need a car—or some other possession—that defines your success and displays it for the world to see. Thus what you consume becomes an outward sign of who you are. The difficulty, however, is that the objects of our consumption are transient and have no lasting value. If my identity, or success, is wrapped up in what I consume—in this case a car—then I must have the newest model at all times lest someone think that I am not at the top of my game or have lost that successful edge. This is not just soulless materialism but, rather, it is a real way in which people use consumption to form their identity and determine how they perceive themselves.

A consumer society is always grasping for new things because any novelty or fresh expression of personal identity temporarily satisfies the longing for self-definition. Once this fades we move on to the next fad, or the next trend, in hopes that we might finally discover what we have been looking for. Underlying each individual's search is an unceasing pressure to be someone else, to be dissatisfied with yourself, and to move rapidly with the flow of the ever-changing world of products. If you are someone who wants gray hair, wrinkled skin, and old clothes you are obviously not much use to the consumer world! Whether it is in fashion, electronics, or other industries, we are relentlessly offered "new and improved" products seemingly on a monthly basis. This is because advertisers understand that if our identities are based on what we consume, then we will always be searching for the next thing since we will never be satisfied with what we have. Creating desire in marketing is essential in convincing people that they need to discard what is old—even if it is still useful—and purchase the new because it is "improved." The goal of the consumer is, therefore, to rise above the dull monotony of what has become passé through incessant consumption so that they might stand out amidst the mass of indistinguishable objects and feel as if they are always on the cutting edge.

When our identities become wrapped up in what we consume, the only way to experience rebirth is to consume even more. In many ways consumerism is a type of spirituality that offers its own framework for what it means to be born again. It is no wonder that shopping malls have often been called "modern cathedrals," because for so many consumers they are a sign of hope that there will always be something new for sale, which means that they will always have the opportunity to consume their way into new life. Shopping offers the lure of new beginnings and resurrection from the old. In his book *Being Consumed,* William Cavanaugh comments on how different brands represent the spiritual aspect of consumerism by creating identities for their products. "Things and brands must be invested with mythologies, with spiritual aspirations; they represent the aspiration to escape time and death by constantly seeking renewal in created things."[7] Yet despite the promises of spiritual fulfilment, the consumer is still left wanting and the yearning in each heart that Augustine spoke of remains unfulfilled.

All of us have probably experienced this at some point or another in our lives. We set out to purchase something and then, if you are like me, you scour the Internet to do research on the product—others could care less about this process and would rather just purchase something without having to think about it. You might read all sorts of reviews on websites that, oddly enough, could have been written by a ten-year-old who has never used the product before! Then, after weighing all your options, you feel the excitement of coming to the buying stage. When the product arrives—or you actually go to a store to pick it up—you delight in the fact that all your hard work has paid off, but soon the glow begins to fade and what you once thought would satisfy your needs is now old and outdated. Maybe you have "buyers remorse" or you experience a sense of disillusionment and emptiness until the process starts again.

At other times we are drawn in by advertising schemes that trigger our irrationality and seek to arouse our emotion rather than sober reason. We have terms like "impulse buying" in our culture because we purchase things without consideration when a desire grows in us that seems too strong to be resisted. If we step back and look closely at the purchasing cycle, we will begin to realize that the desire for consuming often gives us as much pleasure as the gratification of those longings.

Desire is fundamental to modern consumerism and this is why the products we purchase are not designed for value or longevity, but for their potential marketability as being new or different. Why would we be satisfied with version 1.2 when we could have version 3.0? Why would we want a camera that has ten megapixels when we could have one with twenty? I remember doing research when we were about to purchase a pressurized steam iron, and there were some that advertised 3 bars of pressure while others boasted 4.5 bars with variable steam at 120g/min. Of course I had no clue what any of that meant, or what I needed in an iron, but I immediately

7. Cavanaugh, *Being Consumed*, 48.

thought that the one with higher numbers must be better despite the fact that an older model would likely have been suitable.

A consumer society places no value on durability because when new products hit the market, old objects must be disposed of or sold off. Dissatisfaction is followed by disposal. What is old is obsolete and destined for the bin. Consumers create wants—or often have them created for them—and then abandon them after purchases, which creates new wants and new purchases, providing a never-ending cycle of consumption and disposal. This disposable mentality can, unfortunately, creep into other areas of life such as relationships. If we grow tired of someone and they no longer give us that feeling of newness, we can easily ditch them for whoever will make us feel fresh and alive. For the modern consumer, creating a lasting relationship based on love, honesty, and care requires an enormous amount of effort. And it is an effort that many are not willing, or able, to give because relationships require us to relinquish our autonomy, to suffer and endure alongside others, and to share in the joys and sorrows of others as if they were our own. If a person today values the endless consumption and disposal of objects, then the very thought of a relationship based on long-term commitment and mutual love would be terrifying. It would be easier to change one's identity on the Internet and start over rather than suffer through the mental and emotional demands of sharing life with another person. Consumer desire is often met by instant gratification and soon followed by disposal, but relationships require time and effort, which many in today's society are not willing to give.

Since we are constantly being offered opportunities to consume new products, we also find ourselves amidst a culture that has an increasingly short attention span where fluidity and variety of choice trump commitment and faithfulness. This flow of the "liquid modern world," as Bauman calls it, is intensified by the rapid development of Internet and communication technologies.[8] Rather than happening over months or years, trends and fads can change on a daily basis. A video that has gone viral globally one day is replaced by something else the next. And if one's identity is tied to being on the cutting edge of social trends, fashion, or anything else, he/she must be connected to the Internet or social networking sites virtually at all times. Thus we risk becoming dependent on the stimuli of the Internet, TV, etc., that we are saturated with each day.

8. For more on the fluidity of the modern world see Bauman, *Liquid Modernity*.

We are also in danger of overstimulation, which can drown out our own creative abilities and imagination. Instead of taking what we receive in the form of stimulation and allowing ourselves time to digest it—and, in return, produce something that creatively emerges from ourselves—we are apt to become so engulfed in the stimuli that we become desensitized to it. This may all sound a bit exhausting (and it is!), but it is the reality many young people have only ever known. This frenetic pace of life is dictated by a consumer world that shuns the practice of reflection and meditation—unless it can be commoditized and sold on the market—and, instead, ceaselessly produces the next great thing, the next "must have" product that promises to fulfill our desires.

Having examined what lies at the heart of consumerism, we can now turn to some of its effects on our culture. One consequence of the consumer city is an increase in commoditization. Our society can take virtually anything and treat it as something to be bought or sold on the open market. In 2005 a university student auctioned off advertising space on his forehead for the sum of about $37,000. For thirty days the young man wore a temporary tattoo that advertised a snoring remedy and while few might have actually seen his forehead, the worldwide media attention he received provided more than enough publicity for the company's product. He told the reporters, "The way I see it I'm selling something I already own; after 30 days I get it back."[9] This is obviously an extreme example, but it reflects our culture's ability to treat nearly anything as commodity.

This process of commoditization can also be seen in the tourist industry. With the development of inexpensive air travel and other forms of transportation we are able to consume foreign countries like we would any other product. Travel agencies promise that if we spend our hard-earned money on their package deals we will experience tranquility and rest, or fulfill the adventure that we have always wanted. Our expectations are built up so that we go not necessarily to understand a foreign culture, its customs, or its language, but to consume and to satisfy our own desires. For many people foreign destinations are a commodity to be consumed and, if they have paid for their trip, they feel they are entitled to an experience that conforms to their desires. If they are dissatisfied in any way, they will bang down the doors of customer service to make sure they are compensated somehow. Once again we see the sovereignty of the individual consumer

9. Cited in Cavanaugh, *Being Consumed*, 42. For the BBC article online: http://news.bbc.co.uk/1/hi/technology/4170523.stm

who pays for a service and, because he or she has paid, feels entitled to treat other places, or the people serving in those places, as commodities.

Another effect of consumerism is detachment, which, as we shall see, is one of the most significant issues we face in a globalized society. Increasingly we have become a culture detached from the process of production and the producers of the materials we purchase. Cavanaugh argues that since the Industrial Revolution we have moved from subsistence farming and handcrafts to factory labor, which has wiped out cottage industries because of cheaply manufactured goods.[10] We have thus moved from being a society of producers to a society of consumers. Consequently, as production becomes a process hidden from the consumer's sight—and conscience—work itself can be turned into a commodity to be bought or sold. Individual laborers are less likely to be treated as human beings in factory environments because they have become merely one link of many in the production chain.

With the onset of globalization and the shifting of production overseas, consumers have been further severed from the world in which their objects of consumption are produced. This blurring of reality is a powerful tool used to keep the customer from questioning how, or by what means, something was made. Yet an economy detached from its producers leaves us, at times, unknowingly participating in the abuse of others. We might not mean to mistreat a person in Malaysia or Thailand, but the t-shirt we wear may well have been produced by a person working painfully long hours in wretched conditions, making only a few cents a day while trying to keep their family alive. And though we may be vaguely aware that nearly every cheap plastic toy has a "made in China" stamp, we are often cheerfully ignorant, and likely unconcerned, about who has produced what we purchase as we breeze through the checkout counter. Thankfully, in recent years, there has been a move toward ethical consumption and more media attention has been devoted to exposing companies that mistreat overseas factory workers. But despite our best efforts there still remains a significant gap between the things we consume and those who produce them. If you want to test this theory go to your closet, or walk around your home, and see how many things you can find that you know exactly where, and by whom, they were made. If you are like me, you will be hard pressed to find many items you can identify with any certainty. This is not meant to make us feel guilty about what we own, but, instead, it demonstrates how

10. Cavanaugh, *Being Consumed*, ch. 2.

detached we are from the products we use each day. And if we are detached, we are liable to distance ourselves from the moral or ethical implications associated with the commodities we consume.

Everyone is a consumer on one level or another and it is very difficult in our culture to abstain completely from interacting with the marketplace. The question is, however, what kind of consumers are we? Has consumption become part of how we form our identity? Do we have control over our consumption, or do we give in every time we are tempted by the possibility of instant gratification? Do we blindly consume without knowing who has produced the products we purchase? Do we tend to think more about our consumer "rights" than about our responsibility as citizens of God's kingdom? Do our patterns of consumption affect other areas of our life and influence how we understand things like worship and the work of the church? In the next section we shall explore consumerism in the context of worship and what it means to bring our best offering before God.

Offering our Best

When we discuss worship we can, at times, limit ourselves to thinking about what happens on a Sunday morning. But in the context of the Cain and Abel story we see that worship, in the broader sense, is how we offer the best of what we have before the living God. This includes both the material gifts that we bring as well as the offering of a life of faith. We saw above in Gen 4:4 that God looked upon Abel *and* his gifts as a sign of his acceptance, which reminds us of the link between the material and the spiritual in worship. Since we have seen that today's consumerism is marked by consumption that seeks to quench the restlessness of the heart in its search for identity, how, then, does the Christian respond in a meaningful way to express an alternative vision of God's kingdom where one's life and identity is ultimately found in Christ? What will the church look like if it represents a community that eschews the consumer trends in society and enables people to discover who they are in Christ and who they are in relation to one another?

In response to the consumerist utopia that is largely a self-centered world focused on personal pleasure and desire, citizens of God's kingdom can pursue the ascetic life, or the ancient practice of refraining from the pleasures of the material world for the sake of spiritual growth. This may sound terribly frightening to some and if you have had any sort of background in church history, you might immediately recall some of the ascetic exploits of monastics like Simeon Stylites who lived on top of a pillar for nearly forty years! Other stories of superhuman fasts and severe abstinence may also come to mind as acts of celebrated saints from the past. For some Christians these physical feats of discipline smack of a religiosity that appears to elevate human accomplishment over the grace-filled relationship offered through Christ. They question whether practices such as fasting or solitude can be done without trying to earn forgiveness or extort God's favor. Thus they tend to disregard ascetic practice all together. Margaret Miles writes:

> In the theological discourse of our time, the word "asceticism" has become one that collects everything we want to reject in ourselves and in historical Christian tradition. Theologies of embodiment, of play and of sexual identity celebrate the demise of asceticism . . . But an even more unfortunate result of the cavalier treatment of historical asceticism is the loss of ascetic practices as tools for the present care and cure of our own bodies and souls.[11]

When we forsake the practice of Christian asceticism we lose indispensable tools for growth and maturity. And despite concerns about past abuses of ascetic practices, we need not discard them altogether and naïvely think of them as mere remnants of the Dark Ages, which do not apply to our "Enlightened" society. Instead, we can approach the traditional Christian disciplines from the perspective of citizenship—to be a citizen means to adhere to the laws of the land, and in the kingdom of God there is an expectation that each member follow the path of physical and spiritual discipline with the ultimate goal of drawing closer to the love of God and the love of one's neighbor (John 13:34).

There are others, however, who may swing to the opposite end of the pole and exchange the free gift of Christ for a life consumed with rigorous ascetic practice. This path has the potential to overemphasize personal achievements, which could produce false piety and rigid legalism (cf. Col 2:18–23). There is, however, a middle way to be pursued that acknowledges both the complete reliance on the grace of God as well as our human responsibility to train our minds and bodies to make them entirely subject to Christ. So rather than swinging from the extremes of asceticism to doing virtually nothing, I believe there is a need to rediscover a balance of the classical Christian disciplines. While we do not have the space to cover all

11. Miles, "Toward a New Asceticism," 1097.

of the disciplines, in the light of our discussion on consumerism, we shall highlight the discipline of fasting as a radical response to consumption and as a way to offer our lives in worship.[12]

Fasting is one of the great ascetic practices that is often forgotten by many Western Christians. Denying oneself the simple pleasures of food—or other things—might be seen as legalistic or unnecessarily severe, and, if you are like me, can often be circumvented by concentrating on other Christian disciplines like prayer, studying Scripture, charitable giving, and the like. While all these disciplines are, of course, important, they should not be used as replacements for other disciplines—such as fasting. One common misconception about fasting is that it is some somber religious practice where we go about starving ourselves and thinking about how rotten we are with dour faces. Yet the biblical understanding is quite the opposite. Fasting can take place for a variety of reasons, such as mourning or repentance, but it is also meant to open our eyes and our hearts to the suffering of the world around us. Whereas consumerism drives us into our own pleasure-seeking isolation, fasting reveals to us the needs of others and our own need to break from material things that can obscure our relationship with God and with our neighbor. A classic biblical text on fasting is found in Isaiah 58 and is worth quoting in full:

> "Why have we fasted, and you see it not?
>> Why have we humbled ourselves, and you take no knowledge of it?"
> Behold, in the day of your fast you seek your own pleasure,
>> and oppress all your workers.
> Behold, you fast only to quarrel and to fight
>> and to hit with a wicked fist.
> Fasting like yours this day
>> will not make your voice to be heard on high.
> Is such the fast that I choose,
>> a day for a person to humble himself?
> Is it to bow down his head like a reed,
>> and to spread sackcloth and ashes under him?
> Will you call this a fast,
>> and a day acceptable to the LORD?
> Is not this the fast that I choose:
>> to loose the bonds of wickedness,
> to undo the straps of the yoke,

12. For a more in-depth treatment of the disciplines, and the practicalities of how to live them out, I have found Richard Foster's book *Celebration of Discipline* to be one of the best on the subject. See also Dallas Willard's *Spirit of the Disciplines.*

>   to let the oppressed go free,
> and to break every yoke?
>   Is it not to share your bread with the hungry
> and bring the homeless poor into your house;
>   when you see the naked, to cover him,
> and not to hide yourself from your own flesh?
>   Then shall your light break forth like the dawn,
> and your healing shall spring up speedily;
>   your righteousness shall go before you;
> the glory of the LORD shall be your rear guard. (Isa 58:3–8)

This dialogue between the people and God demonstrates the balance between the physical discipline and the attitude of one's heart. The people complain that they have been abstaining from food, but God has not acknowledged their religious devotion. The problem is that they have missed the whole point of the fast because they are seeking their own pleasure and, as a result, have treated those around them unjustly. God explains to them that fasting is about release and freedom. A fast is about breaking the bonds of inequity and bringing us into a caring relationship with our neighbor. Although fasting is an individual—and potentially private—discipline, it is an internal practice that is meant to have external manifestations in our relationship with others and society as a whole. Not only does fasting transform our understanding of who we are in relation to God, but it also reshapes how we think about and treat those around us who are poor and vulnerable.

When we fast we enter into a temporary state of poverty that allows us to identify with those who might be forced to live in poverty on a daily basis. By abstaining from normal pleasures—and especially from food—we become attuned to those who are hungry and in need. As we feel our own stomach pangs we can begin to sympathize, on some level, with those who go to bed hungry every night, or with the homeless person on the side of the road. In the Gospels we are frequently confronted with the call to poverty, but this is not so much an economic statement as it is a reminder that reliance upon material things has the potential to create a rift in our relationship with God and can, consequently, blind us to the needs of our neighbor. Fasting, then, is a way of sounding the alarm bells so that we might be reawakened to the plight of the poor and enter in to meet their needs. This is particularly important in a consumer society where the poor are often excluded because they have no power to purchase and are thus discarded from the mainstream, or forced into labor where they are treated like commodities rather than human beings. Whereas consumerism encourages us to fill ourselves with new things as part of shaping our identity, fasting breaks us from the dull routine of consumption and forces us to re-examine who we are in the light of God and in the light of those who suffer around us.

In the Gospels Jesus says *when* you fast, not *if* you fast (Matt 6:16), because he knew that, as human beings, we "do not live on bread alone" (Deut 8:3; Matt 4:4). In other words, our lives are not defined merely by what we consume, but, rather, our identities are formed in our knowledge and experience of God. Citizenship in God's kingdom today requires us to partake in fasting so we can be released from the self-centered consumer cycle that seeks to discover identity in the never-ending consumption of material things. This may be in the traditional form of fasting from food, but it might also include fasts from clothes shopping or purchases of non-essential items. We might fast from social networking or use of our mobile phones. Whatever it is we choose to give up, when we fast—or abstain from the compulsive habits encouraged by consumerism—we open up time and space for reflection that allows us to stand above the constant stimuli and advertising we absorb each day. And when we fast from food in particular, it is also a way to help us physically slow down. Without nourishment our bodies cannot run at a frenetic pace and we are forced to move about our days in a more unhurried manner. When we slow down we are afforded the opportunity to consider the peace Christ offers to us and to recognize that our true identity is not bound up in the pursuit of "things" but, instead, is found in relationship with God and with our neighbor.

Isaiah writes that fasting is meant to "break every yoke" and while "yoke" is not a word commonly used in the modern world, it presents a vivid image of the burden consumerism can be in a person's life. We can imagine a wooden crosspiece fastened over the neck of an animal and attached to the plow or cart they are meant to pull. The work is laborious and grueling as day after day the animal suffers under the weight of what it carries. So too is the life of the consumer—weighed down by an endless search, chasing fads, purchasing to find fulfillment, but only left with the oppression and emptiness of trying to keep up with an ever-changing world. Yet fasting breaks the yoke and not only releases us from our own burden, but gives us the freedom to liberate others who are oppressed. We are set free so that we might go and feed the hungry, clothe the naked, and care for the weak and vulnerable in our society. This response to consumerism projects a vision of what the kingdom of God, and its citizens, represent—care for the poor, freedom, restoration, and healing—which stands in stark contrast to the self-absorbed, pleasure-seeking life advocated by the consumer city.

Offering our best to God in worship also involves being part of the church as a local expression of the global, universal body of Christ. Consumption is a solitary and isolating activity, but worship in community offers a place where people may come to give and to receive. Yet living in a service-based, consumer culture raises questions about our relationship to the church and whether we are, in fact, more concerned about what we receive rather than what we give. Being labeled and treated as "customers" in so many aspects of our lives, it is easy to begin to blur the distinction between how we relate to those things which we consume and how we relate to others, and to God, in the context of the church. The very word "customer" was once primarily used in the context of economic transactions, but now has spread to other areas of society. We are no longer passengers on airplanes—we are customers. We are no longer patients in hospitals—we are customers. We are no longer students to be educated—we are customers who demand a level of satisfaction. With this type of commodification we have upended the state of relationships that once existed between, for example, the doctor and patient or the professor and student. Rather than a relationship based on trust and respect, there is now an expectation of "customer satisfaction."

This consumer perspective can also influence how we approach our places of worship. If we are giving money to a church—or even if we are not—we may have the expectation that the church somehow owes us some level of satisfaction. Thus we easily can become casual observers, or critics, in worship, searching for something that makes us feel good, rather than actively participating in hopes that we might contribute to the community of believers. If a consumer mentality creeps into our thinking then worship becomes another commodity to be consumed and the local church becomes nothing more than a spiritual supplier that can be discarded, or replaced by a new one, when our desires are no longer being met.

What we are in danger of forgetting is our responsibility as citizens to *participate* in the kingdom of God. When we fail to see our role in the body of Christ, however significant or insignificant, and neglect to express the unique gifts that we have been given to share, we reduce the church to a place of consumption rather than treating it as a dynamic, organic body that thrives and grows on interdependent relationships. Yet when we approach worship in the community of believers as an offering of what Christ has revealed in us, we begin to see the larger painting that God is creating in the local church and in the church throughout the world. We can experience the miracle of contributing out of our own creativity for the sake of building up others and watch in amazement as the gift of one inspires another and sets off a chain of reactions that begin to unveil God's glory. The ecosystem of the church requires each of us to give out of our possessions and out of our experience so that we might draw others into relationships of reconciliation and that we too might be drawn in to receive the abundance of life that comes from the body of Christ.

It is also through worship in the church we can present our material gifts. We noted in the Cain and Abel story the author gives a detailed description of Abel's offering as a sign he brought the very best of what he owned. Abel gave up a significantly valuable possession as a gift to God, while it seems Cain offered something of less consequence. The importance of this sacrificial act of worship speaks volumes to a consumer culture that values debt as a means to purchase more things for the sake of immediate gratification. This is not to say all debt is bad, but unbridled consumption can quickly lead to irresponsible levels of debt and greed, which will ultimately prevent anyone from being able to offer something of value back to God. If we amass significant levels of debt, or if our possessions are being leveraged so that we might consume more, there is little hope of being able to approach the altar with a gift of any import.

To offer our best in worship requires us to critically assess how we are living our lives financially and what material gifts we are offering back to God. To be a citizen of God's kingdom in a consumer culture requires us to live within our means. If we choose to live beyond our means it will have an impact on our ability to worship and contribute to the life of the church or to give to those in need. If what we value is always spent on our own pleasure then we might miss the opportunity to use our finances to benefit others. And if we are using debt as a way to satisfy our immediate desires, we also might not be able to give to those around us who are truly in need. Genesis 4 does not tell us why Cain did not bring the first fruits of his crops, but if he had leveraged his fields in order to take a nice long holiday, he certainly would not have been able to bring his best!

Finally, to offer one's best in worship, as a response to consumerism, is to offer oneself in the celebration of the Eucharist. Cavanaugh writes:

> To consume the Eucharist is an act of anticonsumption, for here
> to consume is to be consumed, to be taken up into participation in
> something larger than the self, yet in a way in which the identity of
> the self is paradoxically secured.[13]

If consumption is the means for forming one's identity in our culture, then
being consumed in Christ is the radical alternative to discovering who we
are truly created to be. When we participate in the Eucharist we accept the
gift of Christ for the whole world as it is represented in his broken body
and poured out blood. We are drawn into the communion of all the saints,
but, as Cavanaugh notes, this does not diminish our individuality. Instead,
it is in this communion that we, paradoxically, discover our unique identity
in Christ. The body of Christ is not some nameless, faceless crowd, but it
is composed of those who participate in the very life of the Trinity and it is
through this participation that one's true name will be revealed.

> To the one who conquers I will give some of the hidden manna,
> and I will give him a white stone, with a new name written on the
> stone that no one knows except the one who receives it. (Rev 2:17)

As Augustine said, all hearts are restless until they find their rest in Christ.
And each heart longs for a sign from God—a sign that conveys his intimate knowledge of our being, even to the deepest recesses of our souls. The
writer of Revelation expresses this sign in the form of a white stone with a
new name written on it. This is no ordinary name, but it is sum of who we
are and who we were created to be. It is a name known only to us and to our
Creator. And through our participation in the Eucharist it's as if that name
on the white stone is slowly being revealed to us as we share in the body and
blood of Christ, and as we are sent out as an offering of Christ to the world.

The Eucharist is an act of remembrance that represents the present
reality of God's kingdom breaking through, and being established, here on
earth. It recalls the mission of God (*missio Dei*) through Christ's death and
resurrection and the continuing mission in the world through the church
and its participation in the transformation of society. As Christ was broken and poured out to bring forgiveness and life, so too the Christian is
broken and poured out to the world through the Holy Spirit as an agent of
healing and reconciliation. The Eucharist reminds us of the ultimate act of
redemption in the world's history and that we too can now participate in his

---

13. Cavanaugh, *Being Consumed*, 84.

redemption by transforming unjust forces in society, by caring for the poor, and awakening the consciousness of the culture to a different way of life.

For citizens of God's kingdom, offering our best in worship may not differ so greatly from what Christians have been doing for centuries or even from what we have seen in the offerings of Cain and Abel. But in a globalized, consumer society, where identity is found in consumption, and the endless din of advertising drowns out the suffering of the world around us, Christians can worship and live in such a way that rejects the self-absorbed hedonism of the culture and embraces the selfless sacrifice and offering of Christ. Whether this is through fasting, prayer and meditation, giving generously, being consumed in the Eucharist, or by other means, citizens of the heavenly city can present an alternative life to the consumer city where one's identity is secured in Christ and is defined by breaking every yoke, caring for the poor and releasing the oppressed. When this is the witness of the church, and of each individual follower of Christ, God's kingdom will be revealed through his people and, as Isaiah says:

> Then shall your light break forth like the dawn,
>   and your healing shall spring up speedily;
> your righteousness shall go before you;
>   the glory of the LORD shall be your rear guard. (Isa 53:8)

4 Am I My Brother's Keeper?

Care for Our Neighbor in a Global Economy

The LORD said to Cain, "Why are you angry, and why has your face fallen? If you do well, will you not be accepted? And if you do not do well, sin is crouching at the door. Its desire is for you, but you must rule over it." Cain spoke to Abel his brother. And when they were in the field, Cain rose up against his brother Abel and killed him. Then the LORD said to Cain, "Where is Abel your brother?" He said, "I do not know; am I my brother's keeper?"

—GENESIS 4:6–9

CHALLENGING THE VALUES OF the consumer city is no easy task for the citizen of God's kingdom. The unquenchable desire for self-fulfillment at the expense of others permeates the air we breathe and yet this ancient biblical story of two brothers offers insights into some of the most basic human responsibilities of care for our brother and sister who God has woven into the fabric of his creation. It is not—and has never been—enough for human beings to look after their own interests without being concerned for those in one's family and for those families who make up one's larger community. In today's globalized society, however, we care for those physically present with us but we also recognize the additional responsibility of caring for those we might never see. There are those who are somehow connected to us through the clothes or food that we buy, the investments we make, or any of the ways that we participate in the global economy. Cain's question, "Am I my brother's keeper?" resonates from the pages of the biblical text and beckons this generation to answer in the light of globalization and economic integration and its impact on humanity. How do we care for our brother and sister in a globalized society? Do our lives and consumption reflect a concern for our brothers and sisters who may be victimized by the global economy? Do we take into account how our daily purchases or investments might affect those around us and those throughout the world? What does it mean to be our "brother's keeper" amidst today's global economic integration?

To get a sense of how Cain's question might address our contemporary global economy, we shall briefly consider some of the economic developments in the West that have led to our present economic situation. As we look at competing economic theories we shall also listen to some of those who, throughout history, have condemned economic injustices brought about by greed and the abuse of technology for the sake of personal gain. And though this historical narrative will be very limited in its scope, I hope it will provide some insight into where we have come from economically— and where we are now—in the context of how we might live faithfully as citizens of God's kingdom in the global economy and how we might fulfill our role as our "brother's keeper." But first we return to our narrative to see Cain's response to his rejected offering and how the ancient interpreters understood this tragic scene.

The focus now shifts to Cain's response and, indeed, the rest of the story highlights his interaction with God. Abel plays a very minor role in the narrative and, as his name in the Hebrew (*hevel*) suggests, his life is brief, vain, and like a mere breath. Even his murder is summed up in a brief sentence (v. 8) and we get the sense that the author is more concerned with Cain's response. When reading any Old Testament narrative it is always important to pay special attention to dialogue since this is often where the biblical authors highlight important characters and themes. In the case of Gen 4:1–16 Cain is the leading speaker and his exchanges with God, before and after Abel's murder, provide the keys to understanding what is central to the story's message.

Cain is deeply offended at being rebuffed by God and his face has "fallen," which is a Hebrew idiom that most likely expresses his indignation, but could also refer to his sorrow or dejection. God responds in a somewhat cryptic fashion and asks why he is so infuriated if, in fact, he could be accepted if he does well. A more literal translation of the Hebrew in v. 7 could read, "If you do well, is there not a lifting up [i.e., forgiveness]?" The Hebrew verb *ns'* (pronounced *nasa*) means "bear, carry, lift," but when used in reference to sin, it can also mean "forgive," as if the transgression is lifted away by God. In this instance it might indicate that Cain, whose face had fallen, will be lifted up, which contains the sense of his being brought back into a right relationship with God (i.e., he is forgiven). The "lifting up" could also be a reference to the acceptance of an appropriate sacrifice, or that God will receive the elder son's gift if he "does well." However we read the meaning of *ns'*, it is apparent that Cain's fate is not completely sealed and God offers him an opportunity to respond by "doing well." The author does not give us any insight into what "doing well" actually means; it may be presenting an appropriate sacrifice or it may be doing good deeds. In either case, at this point in the story, Cain is offered a choice to make amends for his initial failure.

The second half of v. 7 is perplexing even though the English translation above seems fairly straightforward. Despite that fact that the word for "sin" is feminine and does not agree with the verb in the masculine (*rbṣ* is "lie down, rest"), most translations understand the idea of sin lying in wait at the door.[1] Some of the older English translations (KJV, JPS, RSV) maintain the sense of sin "lying" or "couching," while other newer versions (ESV, NASB, NIV) translate with "crouching," as if representing an animal ready to pounce. Still other translations go so far as to say that sin is "ready to attack you," (NCV) or is "waiting at the door to grab you" (NIrV).[2] The problem with these renderings is that when the Hebrew verb (*rbṣ*) refers to animals, it always signifies lying down to rest and not crouching as if ready to attack. A good example is in Ps 23:2 where the psalmist, using the metaphor of sheep and shepherd, says that the Lord "makes me *lie down* in green pastures." Though the difference between "crouch" and "lie" may seem minor, since the narrative is often read typologically, we might question whether sin is an active pursuant (e.g., like the lion ready to pounce in 1 Peter 5:8), or if it is something human beings come across if it is lying in their path. Was Cain ravaged by sin, or did he simply stumble upon it? We know that the end result was the same—Cain sinned and killed Abel—but the manner in which sin is described potentially taints one's perception of the nature of sin and its interrelationship with humanity.

---

1. Some scholars argue that the Hebrew *rbṣ* was borrowed from the Akkadian and refers to a certain type of demon that waited at the doorstep.

2. The shift from "couching" to "crouching" in modern English translations is noted by Gordon, "'Couch' or 'Crouch'?," 195–210.

Another difficulty in the Hebrew comes at v. 8 where there appears to be a gap in the narrative. The text does not recount any words that Cain spoke to Abel, but many of the ancient versions include some sort of dialogue.

> LXX: And Cain said to his brother Abel, "Let us pass through into the field."[3]

> Vulgate: And Cain said to his brother Abel, "Let us go forth out through the doors."

> Peshitta: And Cain said to Abel his brother, "Let us go to the valley."

We do not know why the translators added these statements, but their inclusion may suggest that Cain was purposely luring Abel out, away from Adam and Eve, to a secluded place where he could kill him. In the case of the Peshitta, the invitation to the "valley" relates to early Jewish and Christian tradition that understood Eden as the center of the world set on the highest mountain peak.[4] It was thought that after Adam and Eve were expelled from the garden they descended to live in the foothills. When Cain sought to kill Abel, he took him farther into the valley away from his parents and, metaphorically, away from God.[5]

The killing of Abel farther away from Eden also relates to a theological motif found in the primeval history (Genesis 1–11). Modern scholars have noted a physical distancing from Eden came as the result of humanity's increased sinfulness and alienation from God. What began with Adam and Eve's disobedience and expulsion from the garden led to Cain's fratricide and his ultimate banishment to the land of Nod, East of Eden.

In the Introduction we noted that the Targums were a bit like a modern study Bible, but that their additions and expansions were carefully regulated by the rabbis and were actually incorporated into their translations. One of the most extensive Targum expansions in the Pentateuch comes at Gen 4:8, which fills the gap in the Hebrew text with a detailed conversation between Cain and Abel. With slight variations from the other Targums, Tg. Ps.-J's version explains what transpired before the murder.

---

3. The NIV translates similarly: "Now Cain said to his brother Abel, 'Let's go out to the field.' And while they were in the field, Cain attacked his brother Abel and killed him." The JPS, however, retains the gap: "Cain said to his brother Abel . . . and when they were in the field, Cain set upon his brother Abel and killed him."

4. Brock, *The Bible in the Syriac Tradition*, 24–25.

5. Scarlata, *Outside of Eden*, 116–17.

And Cain said to Abel his brother, "Come, let the two of us go out to the field." And when the two of them went out to the field, Cain answered and said to Abel, "I understand that the world was created in mercy, but it is not guided according to the fruit of good works and there is partiality in judgment. For what reason was your offering accepted with favor, but my offering was not accepted from me with favor?" Abel answered and said to Cain, "The world was created in mercy and according to the fruits of good works it is governed, and there is not partiality in judgment. But because the fruits of my deeds were better than yours, and were first before yours, my offering was received with favor." Cain answered and said to Abel, "There is no judgment, and there is no judge, and there is no other world, and there is no gift of good reward for the righteous and there is no punishment for the wicked." Abel answered and said to Cain, "There is judgment, and there is a judge, and there is another world, and there is a gift of good reward for the righteous, and there is punishment for the wicked." And on account of these matters, the two of them were arguing in the open field, and Cain rose up against Abel his brother and drove a stone into his forehead and killed him.

Various attempts have been made to determine the social and theological context behind the inclusion of the conversation. Some scholars have argued that the debate reflects an anti-Sadducee polemic that can be dated before the destruction of the temple in 70 C.E. The historical split between the Sadducees and the Pharisees was due partially to the Sadducean denial of the resurrection and, therefore, of the concept of punishment and reward in a future world.[6] This is reflected in Cain's words, "there is no judgment, there is no judge, and there is no other world," which portrays him not only as the world's first murderer, but also as the world's first heretic in the garb of Sadducean belief! Others contend that the focus on the absence of judgment, afterlife and recompense, may have been a response to the Epicurean view that the gods have no intervention into human affairs.[7] Whatever the cultural or theological reasons behind the addition, its presence significantly alters the narrative and disconnects us from Cain's cultic transgression and anger. Abel, who is silent in the biblical account, becomes a martyr who professes, and dies for, his orthodox faith. The central theme of his argument against Cain is that God is just and will repay each one according

6. Isenberg, "An Anti-Sadducee Polemic," 441–44.

7. Bassler, "Cain and Abel in the Palestinian Targums," 60–62. For a more in-depth study see Segal, *Two Powers in Heaven*.

to their deeds. This explanation exonerates God from any potential partiality in judgment and shifts the primary significance of the narrative to orthodoxy and the necessity of good deeds. In Tg. Ps.-J. Cain and Abel are no longer treated simply as human beings but, instead, they have become archetypes for the heretic and the true believer.

When we come to the murder scene it is recounted in a mere nine words in the Hebrew. The biblical text does not tell us how Cain killed Abel—though Tg. Ps.-J. says that it was with a stone—and leaves us to imagine the innocent younger brother lying dead somewhere in a field. But his death does not go unnoticed and God confronts the elder brother with a question. Similar to God's inquiry of Adam in Genesis 3:11—"Have you eaten of the tree which I commanded you not to eat?"—his question does not imply that he is ignorant of what has transpired, but, rather, he allows Cain the chance to respond in truth and to take responsibility for his actions. Cain's retort, however, begins with a blatant lie, and his following question portrays his impudence before God. Most modern commentators agree that Cain's impertinence and arrogance is further evidence of the intensification of sin since the departure from Eden. What is also significant in his response is the fact that Cain questions God. If we look at the discourse as if it were taking place in a courtroom, the normal pattern of dialogue would be that God, the judge, has the right to ask questions, but Cain, the accused, is bound by the duty of answering them. Cain, by assuming the "right to ask" in his question to God, turns the dialogue into an inquisition of the divine![8] In a brash reversal, Cain demonstrates his own brazenness with respect to his crime and to the supreme authority of God as his creator and judge.

Cain's question—"Am I my brother's keeper?"—is a clever wordplay since the Hebrew for "keeper" is a term that is also used for shepherds (e.g. Gen 30:31; 1 Sam 17:20; Jer 31:10). So Cain's witty response might be paraphrased, "Am I the shepherd's shepherd?" Yet despite his sarcasm, this question sets the tone for the rest of Genesis, and, indeed, the entire Old Testament, in terms of how we are to relate to those within our own families. The term "keep," however, might sound a bit strange to modern ears as it applies to family relationships. The Hebrew verb ($šmr$) may contain various nuances, but its general meaning is to pay careful attention to something. Adam is commanded to "keep" the garden in Gen 2:15. Moses commands the Israelites to "keep" all the commandments that have come

---

8. Bartor, "The 'Juridical Dialogue,'" 445–47.

from God (Exod 23:13). In 1 Kgs 14:27 it is the guard's responsibility to "keep watch" over the king's door. In all these examples the emphasis is on devoted attention to something that has been entrusted to one's care. When the biblical text uses "keep" within the context of family, we might think more in terms of our duty to our relatives rather than how we feel about them. Cain was not merely to be kind and loving towards Abel, but he was bound by an innate duty to watch over and care for his brother— a responsibility God had built into the pattern of familial relationships.

The notion of paying close attention to, or guarding, members of our family is subsequently expounded on by Jesus in the New Testament on two occasions. In one instance, while he was teaching, his mother and brothers arrived and asked to speak with him. He responded by stretching out his hands towards his disciples and said, "Here are my mother and my brothers! For whoever does the will of my Father in heaven is my brother and sister and mother" (Matt 12:46–50). On another occasion he was questioned by a lawyer who asked, "And who is my neighbor?" (Luke 10:29) In response Jesus tells the story of the Good Samaritan, which emphasizes that all human beings are created in God's image and are deserving of our love and care. Once again Jesus goes beyond the realm of familial duty and highlights the fact that loving our neighbor as our self means we are to keep and care for, not only our brother and sister, but also all of God's children. In some respects, this might have been easier in Jesus's day when care for one's neighbor meant loving those you had personal contact within your local community. Today, however, care for our neighbor extends beyond our immediate physical context to those we affect around the world through our participation in a globalized economy.

ECONOMICS AND ETHICS

To get a better sense of the historical events that have shaped our economy over the past few centuries we shall look at the Industrial Revolution and the economic beliefs of that period, which significantly altered the course of Western history. Theories on how we approach economics, however, were around long before the events of the eighteenth and nineteenth centuries. Economist Amartya Sen contends there are two origins of economic theory he terms the "ethics" and "engineering" approaches.[9] The ethics approach derives from Aristotle's *Nicomachean Ethics*, which describes economics

9. Sen, *On Ethics and Economics*, 3–4.

in relation to its use for politics. According to Aristotle economics has to do with the gain of wealth, but monetary increases should always remain secondary to the greater goal of the enhancement of life: "The life of money-making is one undertaken under compulsion, and wealth is evidently not the good we are seeking; for it is merely useful and for the sake of something else."[10] Aristotle understood that the goal of humanity was not to gain wealth for the sake of personal pleasure, but, rather, that human beings should utilize their resources to benefit the larger community. Thus economics is subordinate to citizenship and wealth is to be used for the common good of the state.

In contrast to this theory is the "engineering" approach, which is characterized by practical issues rather than questions about goodness or truth. It focuses on the "science" of wealth, rather than the ethical questions surrounding the accumulation and use of money, and dates back to writings from the 4th century B.C.E.[11] This approach, characteristic of many modern economists, treats economics as an "objective" science essentially independent of ethical judgments. One might take issue with the claim that any science can be fully "objective," but, nevertheless, these different approaches to economic theory highlight the fact that there was, and continues to be, a debate about whether economics should be governed by ethical behavior or whether it is merely the scientific study of wealth.

In the light of the Industrial Revolution, however, the debate on the nature and ethics of economic practice became even more critical due to the increased scale of manufacturing, increasingly globalized markets, and a widening gap between rich and poor. Such was the case in nineteenth-century England. With a narrow economic ideology and lack of moral leadership among business leaders and politicians, the Victorian period, in many ways, resembled our current financial situation today.

As part of the historical narrative leading up to the present I would like to look briefly at the life and work of John Ruskin (1819–1900)—art critic, social commentator, and prophetic voice of his time—since his life and work is still relevant to contemporary Western society. Although Ruskin did not experience globalization on the level that we do today, he understood the biblical imperative to protect the poor and the vulnerable of society—both at home and abroad—and the responsibility we have as Christian citizens to advocate on behalf of those being disadvantaged by an

10. Aristotle, *Nicomachean Ethics*, I.1–5.

11. For examples see Sen, *On Ethics and Economics*, 5.

economic system devoid of ethics. And while many capitalists will cringe at his idea of a fixed wage and restriction of competition in the market, his words are still appropriate in an age where excessive pay (for some) is the norm and the abuse of wealth is widespread.

Ruskin lived at a time of economic prosperity in England, which was often marred by the exploitation of workers and corporate greed. With the rise of industrialization and increased tension between capitalistic businesses and poorly treated laborers, the Victorian age had to wrestle with social disparities produced by an economic ideology (*laissez-faire*) that is often associated with the utilitarian and individualistic philosophy of John Stuart Mill. By the mid-nineteenth century a stream of opposition to the mistreatment of workers began to take shape and critics emerged from various circles such as novelist Charles Dickens through his work *Hard Times*. Ruskin entered into the political/economic debate with a series of essays called *Unto This Last*. The title comes from Jesus's parable of the vineyard owner (Matt 20:1–16) who generously gave the same wage to the workers hired later in the day as he did to those hired earlier in the day. Ruskin used the text as a complex metaphor to draw attention to the grace-filled economic practices of the vineyard owner in comparison with the socio-economic deficiencies of his day. Despite harsh opposition, Ruskin's economic critique challenged the accepted values of Victorian society with prophetic clarity, and he called for a human ethic in the marketplace in response to the greed that characterized the capitalism of his day. His message speaks volumes to our present economic situation.

In *Unto This Last* Ruskin wrote that economy and society were interdependent and that the *polis*, or "state," rather than the individual, should be central to any economic theory. He emphasized the need for fair distribution and how the nature of one's work should not be directly tied to one's pay. Thus the financial reward for one's work should not merely be based on one's "market value"—as is often the case today—but on a fair wage that does not exceed the worth of one's service to society. And if one's compensation exceeds one's needs, it should be fairly distributed to benefit the *polis*. Ruskin argued that those who seek to become independently rich are only accumulating at the expense of their neighbor's loss and are merely establishing the maximum inequality in one's own favor. Instead, he contends that true wealth is "the possession of the valuable by the valiant" whereby the accumulation of goods must go hand-in-hand with the "valor" of its possessor.[12] The opposite of this is what Ruskin terms "illth," or those whose wealth causes devastation and who become like "pools of dead water" in society.

One of the main themes in Ruskin's economic writing is that the needs of the community must supersede individual gain and wealth, while not intrinsically bad, must never be an end itself but must be appropriated in wisdom for the benefit of others. His goal was to infuse political and economic thought with an ethic based on care and responsibility for one's neighbor and one's nation. There was nothing wrong with a successful capitalist manufacturer who treated his workers fairly and used his earnings for the benefit of the community. What Ruskin abhorred was the individualistic profiteering that had done such damage to the state and the personal welfare of the working classes. It is not difficult to recognize the parallels with the current economic situation and Ruskin's words are as appropriate today as they were in Victorian England.

Having heard Ruskin's critique of his contemporaries, we can now look at some of the economic events that have led to our present situation. Not long after Ruskin's lifetime the U.S., and much of the world, faced another economic crisis in the collapse of the stock market in 1929. The Roaring Twenties was a time of significant prosperity and excess. Many Americans heavily invested in stocks with a high level of speculation and frequently borrowed money from their brokers to purchase even more stocks. When the markets experienced a downturn, panic set in and a massive sell-off ensued, leading to an unprecedented collapse in the market and the start of the Great Depression. Though the exact causes of the crash have been debated, the event, once again, raised questions about the relationship between economics and ethics.

U.S. President F. D. Roosevelt, in his inaugural address (1933), scorned those who had given into "the rules of a generation of self-seekers" and proposed the New Deal, which was not simply about government intervention to provide jobs, but offered structural changes that limited the unbridled greed demonstrated by Wall Street traders. Echoing the thoughts of Ruskin, Roosevelt contended that "Happiness lies not in the mere possession of money; it lies in the joy of achievement, in the thrill of creative effort. The joy and moral stimulation of work no longer must be forgotten in the mad chase of evanescent profits." In other words, as Ruskin wrote, "There is no wealth, but life." Following Roosevelt, however, *laissez-faire* capitalism

12. Ruskin, *Unto This Last*, 82.

maintained its dominance and the "science" of economics prevailed. Questions of right and wrong, just and unjust, became muted in the marketplace and often were treated as private religious matters or questions of personal faith. Unfortunately, as history has demonstrated, human beings left unchecked by laws or regulations—especially in economic spheres—can often bring about social destruction rather than communal harmony. While this is a very brief and select overview of the past two centuries, it hopefully paints a broad picture regarding economic theory and some of the voices that have spoken out against injustice in marketplace.

THE CREDIT CRUNCH AND PARTICIPATING IN THE GLOBAL ECONOMY

When discussing the economic events that have taken place since 2007 the most common popular analysis has highlighted the excessive greed demonstrated by individuals and institutions. Indeed, the public and political outcry against the banks—and bankers—during the credit crunch has been spotlighted frequently in the media. But is their condemnation sufficient as a Christian response to what has happened? Have the bankers become the scapegoat for a widespread greed—as well as other factors—that contributed to the economic crisis? While it is apparent that the recklessness of certain banks was a major factor in the credit crunch, there is also a parallel narrative of individual consumption and debt that played a significant role in the global collapse of the banking system. When we speak of greed, therefore, we must not limit it to certain individuals or institutions, but we must see it as a part of a more pervasive consumer culture that inspired many—particularly in the world of real estate—to tap into a social consciousness that sought individual gain at the expense of others. The question we must now wrestle with, however, is how does the economy of the kingdom of God—and its citizens—function amidst the economy of the consumer city?

One of the most significant shifts in the past decades has been the increase in consumer debt. Recent statistics from the U.S. Federal reserve are staggering. In 2010 the total amount of consumer debt in the U.S. was nearly $2.4 trillion, which means that, according to the 2010 U.S. census, every man, woman, and child in the U.S. has approximately $7,500 in debt.[13]

13. For debt statistics see the U.S. Federal Reserve web site, www.federalreserve.gov and Georgetown University Credit Research Center www.faculty.msb.edu/prog/CRC.

One reason for the excessive rise in debt is the need for instant gratification. Bauman writes:

> A liquid modern setting is inhospitable to long-term planning, investment and storage; indeed, it strips the delay in gratification of its past sense of prudence, circumspection and, above all, reasonability.[14]

With the possibility of experiencing pleasure and gratification immediately through debt, consumers are taught that it is their right to be able to purchase as much as they want with the option of repaying it later. Without weighing the consequences of debt, many are lured into enticing opportunities but will, in some instances, not be able to pay back what they owe.

Prior to the credit crunch banks were gratuitously giving so-called NINJA loans, where people with "no income, no job, and no assets" could borrow significant sums of money. Some of these mortgage lenders offered the promise of home-ownership, a new life, and a new start. People were assured that housing prices would continue to rise and that their investment was all but guaranteed. The reality, however, proved to be the opposite and the dream of settling down and creating a home was shattered for millions across the U.S.—and the world—who are now unable to repay their debt. Not all debt is bad, but it is clear that excessive borrowing for immediate gratification has become a harmful pattern in today's society. Yet despite the damage extravagant debt has caused, most governments of the world condone these spending patterns so that economies might continue to grow and GDPs might continue to rise. How often do we hear the buzzword "consumer confidence" used in the news today as if it is the single most important measure for the state of the economy? If the consumer is not confident—i.e., not demonstrating strong spending habits, or going into debt—then there is little hope for economic recovery.

When we reflect on some of the circumstances surrounding the credit crunch, we can see that excessive levels of debt fed a hunger in the consumer-driven culture that spiraled out of control. And while we cannot go into any great depth on various economic theories, it is clear that the acquisition of wealth was not necessarily the problem leading up to the credit crunch. Instead, one significant issue—among many—was how people acquired wealth through debt for their own fulfillment while neglecting the needs of the community. If, then, the economy of the consumer city is based on

14. Bauman, *Consuming Life*, 31.

instant gratification and the satisfaction of one's desires through the burden of debt, what does the economy in the city of God look like?

In the New Testament Jesus often spoke in parables using economic themes, which did not condemn trade or material gain but often questioned how one used their wealth to benefit others. A good example is the parable of the rich man who hoards his crops, thinking that he will live a long and comfortable life, but then is confronted by the angel of death. Jesus begins the parable with the words "for one's life does not consist in the abundance of his possessions" and ends with the sober judgment, "so is the one who lays up treasure for himself and is not rich toward God" (Luke 12:15, 21). But what does it mean to be rich toward God? I would contend that it means to be rich toward one's neighbor in order to produce a communal shalom. It is true that greed was one of the underlying factors in the credit crunch, but it was not just the bankers—it was anyone who participated in accumulating wealth solely for their own interests rather than looking to the needs of others. In the economy of the heavenly city citizens are called to utilize their resources for the benefit of others. This does not mean that they cannot enjoy individual profits, but they do so only with regard for the wider needs of the community.

It is interesting to note that the term "economics" comes from the Greek *oikonomia*, which essentially means household management or "housekeeping." Inherent in the word is the notion of family and the sense of using resources for the benefit of all who live within a household. The most vulnerable—the youngest and oldest—are nurtured and cared for, those who are strong produce an income to sustain the family, and there is space created for growth, creativity, and the deepening of relationships. Good housekeeping, therefore, requires a balance of all these things to provide stability and common well-being so that the family might flourish and continue to grow in trust and in life. This notion of housekeeping need not break down when expanded to a global level since the fundamental principles of giving and belonging in the common life are still applicable. In fact, good housekeeping reflects a microcosm of how we should live on a macro level. The Chief Rabbi of the UK, Jonathan Sacks, contends that, "Society is the home we build together when we bring our several gifts to the common good."[15]

Rather than merely pointing the finger at the bankers, it would be more helpful to envisage a society that seeks out the good of the community

15. Sacks, *The Home We Build Together*, 240.

in local circumstances—and in global economic policies—to create a place
where human beings are able to thrive in becoming the individuals that
God has uniquely created them to be. As Ruskin writes,

> We need people who . . . have resolved to seek-not greater wealth,
> but simpler pleasure; not higher fortune, but deeper felicity; mak-
> ing the first of possessions, self-possession; and honouring them-
> selves in the harmless pride and calm pursuits of peace.[16]

Thus any economic structure that allows for poverty, injustice, and disad-
vantage to continue to exist must be abandoned and needs to be replaced
by a Christian ethic founded on mutual dependence, giving, sharing, and
inclusion. This is not merely an ideology based on generosity towards
the poor, but it is one that strives for communality and recognizes each
person's worth and their unique contribution to the whole household despite whether they have or have not. How then do we, as citizens of God's
kingdom—and as consumers—become people who seek "simpler pleasure"
and the "calm pursuits of peace" when we participate daily in the global
economy?

As we noted above, many lessons on economics came directly from the
mouth of Jesus when he spoke about the kingdom of God and the establishment of justice and truth in all areas of life—especially in the marketplace.
In the Gospel of Luke alone we find an abundance of examples. The wise
man counts the cost of building a tower or foundation (14:28–30) and, despite commending the shrewd dealings of the dishonest steward (16:1–9),
Jesus condemns those who are lovers of money and place mammon above
God (16:13–14). Proper and wise investment is also commended in the
kingdom (19:11–27). A rich man is justified in having his servants do all
that is commanded because of the nature of their socio-economic relationship (17:7–10), while the tax collector, despite his presumed unjust dealings
with money, will stand justified before God in his repentance above the
Pharisee who does not repent (18:9–14). The need for economic justice
and the act of repentance is strikingly presented in the story of Zacchaeus
who, when called by Jesus, announced that, along with donating half of his
possessions to the poor, he would give back fourfold to anyone that he had
defrauded, which could have been quite a sum of money (19:1–9)! Even
Paul utilizes marketplace language when illustrating the point that he, as

16. Ruskin, *Unto This Last*, 102.

an apostle, is justified in receiving some recompense for his work (1 Cor 9:9–10).

In all of these examples we find a similar theme emerging—economic activity is an integral part of everyday life, but should always be entered into with a spirit of truth, justice, respect, honesty, and fairness where relationship is given priority over profit. When citizens of God's kingdom participate in the economy, therefore, their actions should reflect a principle of right relationship with those engaged in trade and with the communities that surround them. Many of these characteristics mark the spirit of the contemporary "fair trade" or "direct trade" movements that have set out to establish greater equity in international trade. These schemes offer one way in which we can participate in caring for our global neighbor.

At the heart of the Fair Trade movement is the desire to combat some of the unbridled market forces of free trade that have exploited poorer nations in the past and have built up economic structures that can be, in many ways, intrinsically unjust. Buyers of Fair Trade products must pay a minimum price, which aims to cover the cost of sustainable production for the producer so that if market prices fall, the producer is protected. If the market price rises higher above the minimum price, the buyer will then pay the market price. Oftentimes a premium will also be paid by the buyer, which goes toward farm improvements, developing processing facilities, and educational and health care projects. The goal is to produce lasting relationships between the buyers and small-scale farmers in order to ensure the protection of basic human rights, acceptable health and safety standards, and the ability to create sustainable farms that will provide long-term stability. Currently, the most common Fair Trade products are coffee, cocoa, cotton, and rice, but these continue to expand as the Fair Trade movement grows.

One of the outcomes of globalization that was previously mentioned is that we, the consumers, have become increasingly detached from direct transactions with producers. Unlike the previous biblical examples of trade that occurred between two parties, our current environment affords people little opportunity to ever communicate directly with the producer from whom they are purchasing goods. When we enter into a grocery store we do not know where the fruit or vegetables have been grown, how the meat or poultry has been raised, or whether farmers have been given a fair price for the goods we purchase. Likewise, when we enter a store we often have no idea whether the clothing we purchase has been made by a child trapped in slavery or an adult earning a fair wage. The phrase "out of sight, out of mind" aptly sums up the modern consumer in developed countries. Yet for Fair Trade to work consumers must be cognizant of their participation in global markets and whether they are helping or hindering the reduction of poverty by the products they purchase. If we continue to purchase goods that are unethically produced, we are sharing in the injustice that the biblical texts so resolutely condemn and we have failed to care for our neighbor. Thus it is imperative that if Fair Trade—or "direct trade," or any other system that promotes mutually beneficial and just transactions—is to be successful it must begin with our decisions in the supermarkets, clothing outlets, and other stores.

While there are still significant issues that Fair Trade must continually overcome—like defining what a "fair" price is, and the potential power imbalance between the parties involved—it does, at least, provide a way for the consumer to participate in bettering the life of their neighbor who is struggling to survive in the global economy. Ultimately, Fair Trade and other schemes need to be understood in the light of economic and political justice in order to facilitate greater, and more sustainable, development for those who are at the mercy of global markets. If underdeveloped communities participate in the global economy through Fair Trade and yet remain without clean water, education, health care, and a sense of sustainable growth, then the notion of Fair Trade becomes an oxymoron. Thus without vigilance in scrutinizing the Fair Trade markets and the governments or institutions associated with them, we may be at risk of legitimizing increased consumption in developed nations by appealing to the consumer conscience without looking at the deeper issues of social and economic justice.

Fair Trade is, by no means, a perfect answer to alleviating poverty in the global South and caring for our neighbor throughout the world, but it has made significant strides in helping the marginalized through trade and by shedding light on the plight of farmers and communities. It has also reawakened the consumer conscience in developed countries and has enabled consumers to make ethical choices about the products that they purchase while also offering them the opportunity to participate in the growth of poorer communities through their spending patterns. While these are only initial steps towards ending poverty and economic injustice in underdeveloped countries, they are moving in the right direction. If Christians participate in these types of programs, both individually and as communities, they can help relieve the burdens inflicted upon the poor and exploited. They may also engender new questions regarding how believers in developed countries respond morally and ethically to injustice in underdeveloped nations, especially in the light of their own consumption. The hope is that people will not fully be satisfied with the current Fair Trade movement, but will use it as a stepping stone towards establishing God's kingdom of love, truth, and justice in all economic transactions and in every aspect of society.

In the light of bad loans, greed, and the global banking collapse discussed above, citizens of God's kingdom might also participate in the redemption of financial lending through the contemporary microfinance movement. The practice of making small loans has been around for centuries, but one of its modern proponents, Nobel laureate Professor Muhammad Yunus, pioneered experimental credit programs in Bangladesh and set up the Grameen Bank, which continues to service millions of microloans today. Other commercial and non-profit organizations have followed and today hundreds of millions of people living on less than a dollar a day have access to credit that allows them to establish small businesses and work their way out of poverty.

The basic principle of microfinance is to provide small loans to fund entrepreneurs to create, and sustain, viable businesses. The loans typically go to women in developing countries who do not have collateral to secure a loan from a traditional bank or lender. The terms are then established and the repayment plan is agreed upon. When the loan is fully repaid, if the business has been successful, the person may apply for larger loans to expand their operations, which helps the community by providing jobs for others. In many organizations the default rate is less than 3 percent, but larger commercial banks tend to shy away from such loans because of their cost and the ability to make greater sums of money from those with more capital. In the case of some nongovernmental organizations (NGOs), capital is raised through charitable donations, so when the loans are repaid the money can be recycled to provide more entrepreneurs with opportunities to start their own businesses.

When impoverished communities are infused with affordable microloans the increased capital can lead to improvements in roads, buildings, schools, and other essentials like clean water and electricity. As incomes rise, families are able to invest in basic health needs, education, and further development of their businesses. This opens up new doors for hardworking people to move from dependence on foreign—or external—aid to self-sustainability. Part of the United Nation's Millennium Development Goals is to reduce the number of those living in extreme poverty throughout the world by 2015. As an integral part of reaching this goal, the UN designated 2005 as the "Year of Microcredit" because of its significant impact on creating wealth in poverty stricken areas.[17]

Several years ago I traveled to a remote village outside of Addis Ababa in Ethiopia, where I witnessed first hand the transformation that microfinance can bring to a community. Several of the local women had applied for small loans from an NGO to start up cottage industries like making clothing, purses, bags, designing jewelry, and other handicrafts. Many had been successful and nearly all had fully repaid their loans or were in the process of taking out further loans. With the opportunity to start their own businesses, these women had seen a dramatic improvement in their families' standard of living and they were all incredibly proud of their achievements.

Their success had an impact on their community as increased trade brought more people to the village, which allowed for more economic activity and sustained development. One could also clearly see the more intangible outcomes of microfinance in the increased hope of the villagers, the empowerment of women in the community, and the joy of being able to make an honest living through the work of one's hands. In a small Ethiopian village I witnessed something as simple as credit and other financial services—which we often take for granted in the developed world—allowed disadvantaged people to move from everyday survival to stable living. By reducing economic vulnerability through manageable loans, these women had transformed their own lives and the lives of those around them.

It is true that microfinance does not work in all areas and in some places grants, improvements to infrastructure, educational programs, or medical aid may initially be more important. And while microfinance may not be the answer to alleviate all poverty in underdeveloped areas, it offers Christians an opportunity to participate in a project that stands in stark contrast to the suffering and poverty the banking industry recently has brought upon many throughout the globe.

The citizen of God's kingdom lives with both the joys and the burdens that come with participating in the incredible phenomena of globalization. Never before have human beings had such immediate access to goods from

17. For the UN Millennial Development goals see www.un.org/millenniumgoals, and for more on their microcredit emphasis see www.yearofmicrocredit.org. A comprehensive resource on microfinance can be found online at www.cgap.org.

around the world, or been linked together so intimately with others on a global economic scale. Yet because of these developments we are forced to think more seriously about how we live and participate in the economy in the light of Christian faith. Many people, however, find it terribly over-whelming—and inconvenient—to think about doing research on every product they purchase or where their investments are going. To do so would take an extraordinary amount of time and, in the end, might possibly drive us mad. The whole scale of the world economy and its vast complexity can potentially leave us paralyzed in our own decision making as we try to be thoughtful and faithful in our care and concern for our neighbor.

Despite the enormity of the task, however, we can begin with small steps that are as simple as getting on the Internet to do research before we make our next purchase, asking companies where they source their goods, or, if possible, trying to purchase goods from local producers that you can enter into relationship with. If we have pension plans, stocks, or other in-vestments we can research and support companies and organizations that are socially and ethically responsible. Are they working towards creating something of value, or are they only seeking profit? Are they promoting sustainable business models that work for the benefit of society? One only has to search various websites to discover lists of corporations that focus on ethically produced goods, sound business practice, and seek to benefit workers and the environment. Or we might begin to support microfinance institutions or NGOs that have microfinance as part of their development programs. Like anything, it will take time to change our patterns of behav-ior and consumption, but, as we orient ourselves towards Christ, we can begin to place a priority on justice and truth in all of the ways we participate in the global economy.

As we meditate upon Cain's cynical question—"Am I my brother's keeper?"—in the light of globalization and the recent economic crisis, we begin to understand that caring for, and keeping, our neighbor requires us to think in new paradigms about how we participate in the global economy. As one who lives in a developed Western country, I know that I am sheltered from much of the suffering that those in underdeveloped nations experi-ence and yet I also know that I might be unwittingly contributing to their suffering through my consumption or my lack of giving. But if we begin to think of kingdom economics in terms of "housekeeping"—on a global scale—we remember that we are responsible for utilizing our resources for the benefit of every member of the family, especially the most vulnerable.

"Am I My Brother's Keeper?"

Let me close with one last quote from Ruskin, who reminds us of the dangers of greed and affluence and the responsibility we have to care for our brothers and sisters across the globe. "Consider whether, even supposing it guiltless, luxury would be desired by any of us, if we saw clearly at our sides the suffering which accompanies it in the world."[18] The citizen of the heavenly city is aware that every action might have global implications and thus will rethink the daily patterns of their lives in an effort to relieve the suffering and economic injustice experienced by their brothers and sisters throughout the world. Then, as they continue to attune their lives to the heavenly kingdom, they will truly become their "brother's keeper" on a global scale.

18. Ruskin, *Unto This Last*, 104.

5 The Open Mouth of the Earth

Care for Creation

And the LORD said, "What have you done? The voice of your brother's blood is crying to me from the ground. And now you are cursed from the ground, which has opened its mouth to receive your brother's blood from your hand. When you work the ground, it shall no longer yield to you its strength. You shall be a fugitive and a wanderer on the earth."

—GENESIS 4:10–12

AN AVERAGE DAY FOR many of us consists of tasks and travel that often leave us disconnected from the land and from our environment. We might drive in the comfort of our cars, or go by bus, or by train to get to our destinations. We may have to walk or cycle a little ways, but once we arrive at our offices—or wherever we are going—we find ourselves protected in a (climate) controlled environment. Though we might look out the window during the day to see how the weather is doing, we do not feel the strength of the wind, or experience the warmth of the sun, or the wet of the rain upon our skin. We do not smell the richness of the soil after harvest, or the blossoming fruit trees, or the freshly cut grass of the fields. Instead, most of us are confined to comfortable spaces throughout the majority of our day, which sever us from cycles of the natural world.

When it is time for lunch we might purchase something from the cafeteria or bring something we have bought in the store, but we do not know where the food has come from. We just assume that it will be there everyday despite what is happening in the world. We might hear of droughts or flooding, but it has little effect on how we go about our daily lives. If we visit the grocery store on the way home, we expect that the aisles will be stockpiled and usually there are more brands and items than we could possibly imagine. We do not know how the food has been produced, what has gone into it, or where it has come from, but most of the time we put it into our carts without question. By the time we get home in the evening, we have travelled through the elements unscathed to our (climate) controlled houses or apartments. We switch on the lights not thinking about where our energy comes from and relax before we go to bed.

This may not be the typical day for everyone, but, if you are like me, this tends to be how we go through life—unaware of the natural rhythms of the land, ignorant of where the food and resources we consume come from, oblivious to how we are affecting the environment by our lifestyles, and yet all the while enjoying the luxuries and high standard of living that we have achieved in the Western world. One practical consequence of our thought-less consumption of natural resources is the negative impact we are having on the environment. On another level, however, our indiscriminate treat-ment of the earth raises theological questions regarding our relationship to the land and its role in God's plan of salvation. Is there a direct connection between Christian discipleship and how we treat the land? Do our lifestyles demonstrate humility and respect for the roles God has given us within the community of his creation? Reflecting on the average day described above one would be tempted to say that they do not, but this raises a significant dilemma for the contemporary citizen of God's kingdom—how can one express their faith by living according to the patterns God has designed for humanity within creation? What does it mean to be entrusted with the responsibility of caring and keeping the land, which is an active partner with humanity in the cosmic plan of salvation?

In the previous chapters we noted the effects of globalization on re-lationships, consumption and identity, and economics, but another aspect of our culture that has changed profoundly since the Industrial Revolution has been our relationship with the land. This includes both our extraction of resources from the earth and our utilization of the land for the mass production of food that is traded on the world markets. Recent history has shown that our extensive and careless use of the land has led to air and wa-ter pollution, excessive waste, suburban sprawl, deforestation, and deserti-fication. The typical attitude behind such treatment of the earth's resources has been to think of the land as an inexhaustible—and forgiving—account that will give us its yield at our every command without ever requiring us to make a deposit. We have assumed that all natural habitats are for our benefit and that we can do with them as we please for the sake of human progress. Such thinking has led to the ecological crisis of our age and while there are still many who disparage the very notion that there is a crisis, it is clear that, with a world population that has nearly doubled in the past forty years and a greater demand for natural resources, we are coming to a tipping point when the account we have carelessly tapped into may soon run dry. So how might the Cain and Abel story—and the rest of Scripture—speak to our present ecological challenge?

When we return to our ancient story we come to a scene of confrontation where we are introduced to another character in the narrative that will play a significant role in Cain's punishment. Having provided Cain with the opportunity to confess, God now exposes the elder brother's bloodguilt by revealing that, though dead, Abel still cries out from beyond the grave. The earth, or ground, has "opened its mouth" to receive Abel's life. The sound of innocent blood shed upon the earth, though silent to humanity, echoes in the courts of heaven, appealing to the divine Judge. The narrator paints the picture of both the earth and Abel standing side by side, as if in a courtroom, to protest the injustice committed by the elder brother. Indeed, even the language of the Hebrew suggests that Abel's "cry" is a plea for God's justice since the verb is often used throughout the Old Testament by victims of oppression seeking divine intervention (cf. Exod 22:22, 26).

The interpretation of Abel's blood pleading for justice is later expressed in the apocryphal book of Enoch where the angel Raphael escorts Enoch to a place where the spirits of the deceased wait for the final day of judgement. Enoch hears the voice of one imploring God for justice and asks who is speaking. Raphael responds, "This is the spirit which came out from Abel, the one whom his brother Cain murdered. And Abel makes his suit against him until his seed is destroyed from the face of the earth, and his seed is annihilated from among the seed of men" (1 En 22:7). The author of the letter to the Hebrews might be alluding to this when he writes that Abel, "though he died, still speaks" (Heb 11:4) and later describes Jesus as the mediator of a new covenant whose sprinkled blood "speaks a better word than the blood of Abel" (Heb 12:24). The comparison is probably that Christ's blood speaks a word of forgiveness, while Abel's blood cries out for justice.

Some rabbinic interpretations highlight the fact that the Hebrew word for blood in Gen 4:10 is plural and could be translated "bloods." In the

Mishnah (*m. Sanh.* 4.5) the rabbis argue that, in a capital case of murder, the blood of the victim and their offspring will remain upon the head of the guilty forever. Appealing to Gen 4:10 they write, "It does not say, 'The blood of your brother' but, 'The bloods of your brother'; his blood and the blood of his descendants." For the rabbinic interpreters a murder reflected not only the loss of the individual life, but also the loss of generations of descendants who have been deprived of their existence.

Thus far in Genesis the snake has been cursed (3:14) and the ground has been cursed (3:17), but this is the first instance where a human is cursed.[1] According to Mosaic Law the punishment for murder was the death penalty (Exod 21:12), but, rather than suffer death, Cain is cursed from the ground. The rabbis, however, argued that Cain was guilty of homicide, and not of murder, because he did not know his blow would take the life of Abel.[2] Whether the murder was intentional or unintentional, we do not know, but it is apparent that Cain will be banished from the land that formerly sustained him. In this context the "ground" probably represents the cultivated soil and Cain, who tainted the soil with his brother's blood, will no longer live by the produce of his labor but will be driven from the very elements that once gave him life. It is important to recall that, in the primeval history, human beings are understood through, and in many ways are defined by, their intimate relationship with the earth. Thus Cain's punishment might well have been considered worse than physical death since he will experience alienation from God and from his occupation in tilling the earth. Instead, he will be a fugitive and a wanderer. Even Adam, despite the curse upon the earth in Gen 3:17, remained a tiller (Gen 3:23), but Cain, as Augustine writes, is the founder of the first city (Gen 4:17) and nothing more is said about his farming. He is condemned to a life as a "fugitive and wanderer on the earth," which we shall discuss in greater detail in the next chapter.

For now, however, the narrative focuses on Cain's relationship to the earth and how it will no longer yield its fruits to him. The land becomes a participant in the curse and no matter how hard Cain tries, it will not bear a harvest for him in accordance with God's sentence. Cain is alienated from God, and from his source of life, because he has committed the greatest of sins—he has destroyed another human being made in the image of God.

1. See Westermann, *Genesis* 1–11, 306.
2. *Gen. Rab.* 22:26.

The Covenant Relationship Between the Land and God's People

While the ancient interpretations and translations highlight the nature of Abel's plea and his poured out blood, they do so in relation to the land. It is here that the biblical narrative raises the issue of the land's relationship with humanity and its participation in the greater narrative of God's relationship with his people. That the earth is personified in this portion of the story reveals an important biblical truth—the earth, and all of creation, is integrally linked to the salvation history of humanity.

Later in the biblical narrative we discover that the land is an essential participant in the covenant made between God and Israel. When God delivers the Israelites from Egypt he promises that he will grant them a land of abundance where they will dwell in accordance with his covenant (Lev 25:23). This underscores the fact that God remains the owner of the land in perpetuity. Israel has no inalienable right to the land, but they may live there only insofar as they are obedient to the covenant. Yet the land is not passive in its covenant role and does not sit by idly while human beings commit all types of atrocities. Instead, it bears witness against those who have transgressed the moral fabric that God has revealed in creation and covenant. Thus the earth can act as the agent of God's judgment as it does in Num 16:32 where, with similar language to Gen 4:11, we are told that the earth "opened its mouth" to swallow up everyone that belonged to the household of Korah. The earth can also be polluted and profaned by humanity when unjust blood is shed upon it (Num 35:33) or when people worship false gods (Jer 3:9). In fact, the whole of creation can suffer because of humanity's sinful behavior and this might be best summed in the words of the prophet Hosea:

> Hear the word of the LORD, O children of Israel,
>> for the LORD has a controversy with the inhabitants of the land.
> There is no faithfulness or steadfast love,
>> and no knowledge of God in the land;
> there is swearing, lying, murder, stealing, and committing adultery;
>> they break all bounds, and bloodshed follows bloodshed.
> Therefore the land mourns,
>> and all who dwell in it languish,
> and also the beasts of the field
>> and the birds of the heavens,
> and even the fish of the sea are taken away. (Hos 4:1–3)

The vision that Hosea describes is one of severe drought that comes upon the land because of the people's lack of knowledge of God and their disobedience to the covenant. Though they do not follow the exact order of the Ten Commandments, Hosea's condemnation of their cursing, lying, murdering, stealing, and adultery clearly recall the laws given to Moses on Sinai. As a result of their unfaithfulness the land "mourns," which could also be translated "languishes" or "dries up." Creation suffers as a consequence of humanity's sin and the moral depravity of human beings brings destruction upon the creatures of the earth. When humanity abuses its relationship with the land and rejects covenant obedience, creation is afflicted. Hosea ends this passage with a virtual exclamation point by saying that, because of the sins of the people, the drought has become so terrible that even the fish of the sea are dying (cf. Jer 4:22–27)! This affirms, as Christopher Wright argues, that God's covenant relationship with Israel is, indeed, not between two parties, but is triangulated between three—God, Israel, and the land.[3]

This web of relationships must be maintained in order for covenant blessings to be made manifest and it begins with the most basic unit of society—the family. Thus the fifth commandment states, "Honor your father and mother, *so that* your days may be long in the land that the Lord your God is giving you" (Exod 20:12; Deut 5:16). It is the only one of the Ten Commandments that contains a promise and demonstrates that covenant obedience within one's household was a requirement for a long and flourishing life in the land. Responsibility and care for creation begins in the home and our fostering of right relationships with those closest to us.

In contrast to the earth that languishes because of the people's rejection of God's law, the Old Testament is filled with examples of the earth's fertility and fecundity when the covenant relationship remains healthy. This is summed up in Lev 26:3–5:

> If you walk in my statutes and observe my commandments and do them, then I will give you your rains in their season, and the land shall yield its increase, and the trees of the field shall yield their fruit. Your threshing shall last to the time of the grape harvest, and the grape harvest shall last to the time for sowing. And you shall eat your bread to the full and dwell in your land securely.

When God's people demonstrate their love through covenant obedience we find extravagant images of a land that bursts forth with fruitfulness. The psalmist declares that truth will spring up from the earth and that

3. Wright, *God's People in God's Land*, 104–5.

righteousness will look down from the sky and the earth will increase its yield when the glory of the Lord dwells in the land (Ps 85:10–12). This pattern is also reflected in Psalm 72, which is a prayer for the king to rule according to justice and righteousness and to defend the cause of the poor and needy against the oppressor. When this happens, the fields will produce an abundance of grain and the earth's fruitfulness will be like that of Lebanon and all the peoples will be blessed (vv. 16–17). Indeed, this is exactly what happens in Psalm 147 when the king is God who rules justly over the people and provides in abundance for all of his creation. It is through his gracious rule and covenant love that the earth responds joyfully and celebrates with humanity in the form of agricultural productivity.

While covenant obedience depicts one aspect of humanity's relationship with the land, the intimate connection between human beings and creation is nowhere made more explicit than in the first three chapters of Genesis. Let us briefly look at the cosmic account of creation in Genesis 1 and then move to the more "earthy" account of Genesis 2 to draw out some of the biblical themes that speak to the whole of the human race and their responsibility within the community of all living things.

THE CREATION ACCOUNT OF GENESIS

The book of Genesis begins with a magisterial, cosmic symphony orchestrated by the very sound of God's voice. He calls the world into being (Rom 4:17; 2 Pet 3:5) through speech, and by his word fertility, blessing, and order triumph over chaos. Whereas the ancient Babylonian creation account in the Enuma Elish tells of Marduk's battle with and destruction of Tiamat, the God of Genesis demonstrates supreme authority from the outset. Yet it is clear that despite the authority God possess over the universe, he is not depicted as authoritarian. The Author of life is the artist, scientist, musician, and poet who brings into harmony the whole of creation in the opening verses of Genesis 1, and it is within this accord that human beings have been uniquely placed with a particular commissioning. It is no small thing, therefore, for Christians to profess with the Apostles' Creed, "I believe in God, the Father almighty, creator of heaven and earth," since this declaration is an acceptance of the belief that we live and dwell in a corporeal world that was formed and shaped by the hands of the God we worship. Thus our treatment of his creation is of the utmost importance because our use of the earth ultimately demonstrates either our love, or contempt, for the Creator.

Some commentators, however, contend that the Christian doctrine of creation advocates human control over the environment, and that the world primarily exists for the sake of human beings. L. White concludes that this theology is one of the root causes of Western exploitation of the environment and that Christianity "bears a huge burden of guilt for environmental deterioration."[4] His thesis, however, has little to do with the actual interpretation of Gen 1:26–28, and what it means for humans to "rule over" and "subdue" the earth, but, instead, is based on historical interpretations within the Christian tradition. While it is true that some Christian theologies may have contributed to harmful Western attitudes towards nature, the most significant factor in the abuse of the land emerges from the modern scientific movement in the seventeenth century. With the onset of modernity we find the emergence of more literal readings of Scripture and we encounter biblical arguments being made for aggressive engagement with nature.[5] These "exploitations," however, were often motivated by the belief that humanity, through scientific advancements, could redeem the earth from the curse of Gen 3:17. Thus the historical Judeo-Christian record, while at times demonstrating a desire to harness latent capacities in nature, does not support the claim that certain religious beliefs have directly influenced attitudes of control, abuse, and despotism over the environment. Despite some of the unfortunate developments and theologies that emerge from the Enlightenment period with regard to human domination over the natural world, we shall see that the Genesis narrative itself promotes a more ecologically sensitive picture of humanity's role and place within the created order.[6]

The first description of humanity comes in Gen 1:26 where human beings are distinguished from the rest of creation by being made in the "image" and "likeness" of God. Without tracing the vast sum of scholarship on the *imago Dei* ("image of God"), we can begin by noting that the language of "image" is probably rooted in the royal ideology of the ancient Near East. Some scholars contend that bearing the image of God corresponds to the notion of the king as God's viceroy upon the earth. This theory is largely based on the Egyptian and Mesopotamian description of the king as one created in "the image of God." The Pharaoh's identity as God's

---

4. White, "The Historical Roots of our Ecological Crisis," 1207.

5. See Harrison, "Having Dominion: Genesis and the Mastery of Nature," 17–31.

6. See Murray, *The Cosmic Covenant*, for a more in-depth look at the Old Testament's understanding of God's covenant with humanity and the land.

representative on earth is summed up by Amon Re's words to Amenophis III: "Thou art my beloved son, come forth from my limbs, my very own image, which I have put upon the earth. I have permitted thee to rule over the earth in peace."[7] If the language of "image" in Gen 1:26 is promoting the ancient Near Eastern idea of royal authority upon the earth, then this cannot include despotic rule. What is central to the notion of a human being acting as God's viceroy is the demonstration of authority insofar as it represents the character of the heavenly king/god and establishes a kingdom of peace. In the biblical text, therefore, bearing God's image carries with it the responsibility to emulate the Creator who always displays love, mercy, and justice in his relationship with the creation. And, furthermore, we note that the royal language of being created in God's image in Genesis is not reserved for the highest political ruler of the land, but is ascribed to every man and woman!

Others have taken the *imago Dei* to mean that humans contain a likeness to God in spiritual or moral capacities, or possibly in physical form. In this understanding the force of the text is to distinguish human beings in their relation to God and their place in creation. Karl Barth sums up this view: "It does not consist in anything that man is or does. It consists as man himself consists as the creature of God. He would not be man if he were not the image of God. He is the image of God in the fact that he is man."[8] However we understand the meaning of bearing God's image, it is clear that human beings have been set apart among the created order in Genesis to be in special relationship with the Creator, and it is out of this relationship that humanity is given its awesome authority and responsibility within the natural world.

After being fashioned in the divine image, God commands human beings to "rule over" the fish, birds, livestock, and "every creeping thing." The Hebrew word for "rule over" is often used in the context of a king's rule (e.g., 1 Kgs 5:4 [4:24]; Isa 14:6; Ezek 29:15; Pss 72:8; 110:2). Human beings are not meant to abuse their royal authority and exploit that which is under their dominion, but, instead, they are commissioned to govern over it in the same manner that the divine King governs over the universe—with love, justice, and compassion. Yet we must be cautious in how far we extend the viceroy metaphor because that which is created does not wield the identical power of the Creator. R. Bauckham argues, "The close relationship between

7. Westermann, *Genesis 1–11*, 153.
8. Barth, *Church Dogmatics* 3/1:184.

the image of God and the dominion means that the latter is an exercise of rule *on behalf* of God, not *instead of* God."[9] Thus human "dominion" cannot be taken to mean that human beings are above the created order, but, instead, they are part of the community of creation, participating in the shared life of all things.

In Gen 1:28 it is reiterated that humans should rule over the creatures and "subdue" the earth. While it is true that the Hebrew *kabash* is frequently used with negative connotations, when "subdue" is used in reference to the land it often refers to possession with the sense that a certain locale may be inhabited and cultivated (e.g., Num 32:22, 29; Josh 18:1; 1 Chron 22:18). Thus it is a uniquely human endeavour to tend to the land in such a way as to make it bear fruit to sustain and allow for the further procreation of humanity. This obviously raises important questions regarding the practice of genetic manipulation of food sources. Without dismissing the possible benefits of scientific advancements, the biblical ethic does not condone the insidious treatment of the world for one's own advantage, as if we were gods with the authority to do as we see fit. The author of Genesis could not have envisaged an age of genetic modifications in agriculture—or in human beings—but the text does provide a paradigm of human responsibility within the community of creation that does not supplant or undermine the creative power and authority of God.

In the New Testament Jesus offers a similar paradigm for human authority over creation by using the metaphor of a shepherd and his sheep. The sheep will follow the shepherd because he calls to them and they know his voice and they trust him (John 10:3–5). Unlike the hired hand that runs at the first sign of danger, the good shepherd lays down his life for his sheep (John 10:11) because he loves and cares for his flock. There is an implied intimacy and understanding in the metaphor that can extend to our own relationship with the world around us. Jesus is the shepherd-king who, though having dominion over all things, uses his lordship to serve and give his life for his sheep. The shepherd's relationship with his sheep is, therefore, one of authority and sacrificial love—he rules over his flock not as a tyrant, but with compassion and love. We cannot underestimate the theological importance of how humans rule over, care for, and live as participants in the community of creation in both the Genesis narrative and in the language of Jesus. All human beings, no matter what race or religion, are given the awesome responsibility of shepherding and tending

9. Bauckham, *Bible and Ecology*, 30.

to the natural world. Though we may or may not choose to use the language of "stewardship," our relationship to any living creature should be marked by the beneficent power that is demonstrated by God, the Creator of all things, and by his Son, Jesus Christ.

In Genesis 2 the lens of the creation narrative narrows and the focus turns to Eden and its first dwellers. The story depicts God, the potter, who shapes the first man from the "the dust of the earth" (v. 7) and breathes into him the breath of life, which is a familiar motif in other ancient Near Eastern creation myths. Since the constituent parts of human beings are both divine (i.e., God's breath) and mortal (i.e., dust), they are uniquely bound to both God and to the earth. There is no division in the creation account between the "spirit" and "flesh," but the two are inseparably joined. Thus we cannot speak about a "spiritual" relationship with God without also speaking of our relationship to the earth and to all of creation.

God moves from potter to gardener and plants a garden in Eden where he places Adam (Gen 2:8, 15). Though Eden has often been called "paradise" (a loanword from Persian translated by the Greek *paradeisos*), the concept of a perpetual state of bliss amidst Elysian Fields is completely foreign to the Old Testament. Adam is placed in a garden with the specific mandate to "till it" and "keep it." Work, or caretaking, is an essential part of humanity's role within creation. Without work life would not be complete and human beings would not fulfill their vocation to enhance and tend to the natural resources that God has provided. The Hebrew word choice is significant because "till" implies the act of creating with land that remains uncultivated and unproductive, and "keep" implies the conservation and care of the resources that are used. The acts of tilling and keeping are not static, but, instead, they represent a commissioning for humanity to continuously engage in industry and preservation, following the pattern set by God with a balance between work and rest. Later on God commands the Israelites to allow the land to rest, which meant that it was to lie fallow in the seventh year as a "Sabbath to the Lord" (Lev 25:2–3). In fact, rest for the land was intimately tied to the punishment of exile since the Israelites refused to let the ground lie fallow (Lev 26:32–35). We can see, therefore, that the creation narrative of Genesis 1–2 is not to be seen as a series of acts confined to the beginning of the cosmos, but, rather, it inspires a vision for the ongoing process of tilling and keeping that humanity has been appointed to participate in.

Despite the ecological harmony found in the original order of creation as witnessed in Genesis 1–2, the Edenic ideal of the communion between human beings and the natural world does not last. In Genesis 3 discord arises from deception and disobedience, and the possibility of ecological accord is dashed. Though we do not have the space to examine in detail the effects of the choices made in Eden, the biblical narrative is unambiguous in its insistence that the relationships in creation that were established from the beginning have been broken. Whereas Adam and Eve were meant to experience blessing, they are now condemned to suffer (Gen 3:15–19). And though the earth was designed for fertility and fecundity, it is now cursed to bring forth thorns and thistles from human labor. We cannot, however, conclude that the situation is irreparable, or that peaceableness and congruity cannot be achieved between humans and the natural world. Though we have only examined the first few chapters reflecting on the original creation and its subsequent brokenness, as well as the tragedy of Abel's innocent blood being swallowed up by the earth, Genesis 1–11 encourages us to look forward to the history of Israel and the work of reconciliation and restoration begun in Abraham (Genesis 12), completed in Christ, which is now to be enacted by the church (2 Cor 5:18–20). Within this framework, it is vital that citizens of the heavenly city understand their responsibility as caretakers of creation in an increasingly globalized and complex world.

Having examined the creation account we can conclude that human beings have been uniquely created in the *imago Dei* with a viceroy-like authority over the natural world that should reflect the character of the divine King. Humanity has been commissioned to create with the land and to care for it, not as if they are above it, but like ones working within a community—giving, taking, sharing, helping and not exploiting for selfish reasons. Bauckham writes, "It becomes clear that the Bible's meta-narrative assumes that humans live in mutuality with the natural world, not domination, and especially not with the aim of emancipation from nature, but in complex mutuality."[10] Despite the fact that this original relationship has been broken, the biblical story of human history in relationship to the rest of creation is one of reconciliation and renewal. This work of reconciliation is achieved in Christ through whom and in whom all things are reconciled (Col 1:19–20). The very nature of Christ's physical body after the resurrection is a sign and promise of resurrection for human beings on earth, in the natural world, and not in some disembodied Platonic state in the

10. Ibid., 150.

heavens. The kingdom of God will come "on earth as it is in heaven" and, as Moltmann contends, "that is why a resurrection of nature too will not lead to the next world, but into this-worldliness of the new creation of all things. God does not save his creation for heaven; he renews the earth."[11]

THE LAND: FROM SACRED TO SLAVE

In an age of scientific advancements, globalization, and a burgeoning world population, it is imperative that a theology of creation care emerges with a clear sense of the past, present, and future hope for both humanity and nature in the light of future resurrection. Unfortunately, much of the recent debate on the environment has centered on the question of climate change and global warming. Though these are urgent issues that must be addressed, they are not, and should not be, the primary reason for a Christian's engagement in creation care. The biblical imperative that we have outlined above calls citizens of God's kingdom to a life that is consciously and steadfastly aware of one's responsibility to care for and keep the land in a way that reflects the character of the Creator. This means that, despite technological developments, we still adhere to the fundamental principles of tilling and keeping, resting and working, and remembering our relationship of interdependence within the whole of creation. Human beings have not been placed in some sterile, colorless environment, but, rather, we live amidst a world teeming with fertility and life that requires us to play our role as caretakers because our very existence is bound to it. And while the biblical text does not provide us with direct applications to address our current ecological crisis, it does give us a paradigm grounded in real hope for a future where faith, life, and the land coexist in a spirit of shalom.

As we reflect on our biblical story, two particular criticisms of Cain illustrate how some ancient interpreters understood humanity's relationship with the land and also provide an appropriate critique of some agricultural practices today. In his commentary Philo described Cain as one who was full of impiety and greed, which was summed up in his name (the Hebrew for "Cain" means "acquire, possess"). Philo went on to say, "For instead of thinking that all possession belonged to God, he conceived that they all belonged to himself" (*Cherubim* 65). Another ancient Jewish interpreter, the historian Josephus, argued that God delighted in Abel's gift (the firstborn of his flock) because it was naturally grown, but rejected Cain's offering

11. Moltmann, *Sun of Righteousness, Arise!*, 72.

because it was greedily procured by forcing it from the ground (*Ant.* 1:53–54). How exactly Cain forced his crops to come up is not explained, but Josephus's point is that Cain demonstrated his wickedness by not allowing the earth to produce its fruit in due season. Instead, he was impatient and, rather than letting the land give its yield in its own time, we get the sense that he violently stripped the land for his own selfish purposes. These criticisms of Cain—demonstrating his greed and disregard for the natural rhythms of harvest—could equally be applied to contemporary industries that seek to exploit the land, or livestock, for their own gain. The poet and agrarian Wendell Berry sums this up when he compares the attitude of commercial industries with that of the ideal of a farmer:

> The exploiter is a specialist, an expert; the nurturer is not. The standard of the exploiter is efficiency; the standard of the nurturer is care. The exploiter's goal is money, profit; the nurturer's goal is health—his land's health, his own, his family's, his community's, his country's. . . . The exploiter wishes to earn as much as possible by as little work as possible; the nurturer expects, certainly, to have a decent living from his work, but his characteristic wish is to work *as well* as possible. The competence of the exploiter is in organization; that of the nurturer is in order—a human order, that is, that accommodates itself both to other order and to mystery.[12]

In the eyes of some ancient interpreters Cain was an exploiter who neither had regard for the land nor for the gift of life that it produced. In a similar manner, it might be said that our treatment of the land today reflects a human arrogance that prides itself on control and manipulation for the sake of efficiency, production, and profit. This drive for human autonomy and independence, rather than interdependence, demonstrates our desire to have dominion over the land in a way that perverts the command of Gen 1:28 and ignores our place *within* creation. But how did we get to this point in history? How has the land moved from being sacred—filled with the mysteries that bring forth the physical necessities and joys of life—to being our slave and treated like some industrial machine that is useful only when it produces on demand?

While we do not have space to examine every aspect of modern life that relates to the environment, in the following we shall look at a few examples of how we have become estranged in our relationship to the land and how we have perverted the biblical ideal for our participation in the

12. Berry, *The Unsettling of America*, 7–8.

community of creation. Once again we note the theme of detachment in our globalized society. We have seen alienation in contemporary relationships, in consumption, in the global economy, and now in our connection to the earth. In this discussion, however, I do not wish to present a full-scale attack on technology. Advancements in areas of production are not always intrinsically bad and some should not be abandoned. For technology is not, necessarily, the enemy of creation, but can assist in sustainability that makes life possible. Instead, we can utilize technology by subjecting it to the moral lens of Scripture and judge whether its use is leading humanity and creation towards redemption, or if it is leading towards destruction. The hope is to illuminate points where our culture has distorted the original role we are to play amidst creation so that we might, as citizens of the heavenly city, live in ways that demonstrate what it means to care for and keep the earth in accordance with the rule of a gracious king.

In chapter 4 we spoke about the Industrial Revolution and its effects on the globalized economy and the commoditization of the workforce. During that same period (eighteenth to nineteenth century) we find the growth of urban societies and the increased capacity for mass food production on a scale previously unknown. The outcome was a movement away from the agrarian life—as it was once practiced—and, consequently, a distancing from the intimate relationship with the natural cycles of harvest, death, and new life that come with the care and tilling of the land. Urban dwellers became sheltered from these rhythms of nature because they no longer directly affected their day-to-day lives. Rain became a mere inconvenience for those in the city rather than being seen as the most crucial element to support life. Thunderstorms, hailstorms, or other forces of nature were passing spectacles viewed through a protective window from the comfort of one's home. Urban dwellers moved away from participating *in* creation and became spectators *of* creation, if, that is, they decided to acknowledge the natural world in their daily lives at all. This transformation of urban centers promoted a sense of power and trust in the machines that govern daily life rather than a sense of humility and susceptibility to the cycles and unpredictable events of the natural world. Rather than working with the land and understanding the processes of life and growth, we began to see the land as an inanimate machine that could be manipulated for the end goal of production. This is not to idealize our ancestors' agrarian life, which had its own issues and hardships, but, rather, we can point to the obvious disconnect from the land that occurred when mass food production could sustain sizeable populations in urban centers. Similar situations and issues arose in ancient cities like Rome, but the scale of urban life today is unlike anything we have experienced in history thus far.

We find a similar disconnect from the land in many urban and suburban centers today, and an ignorance of how one's life affects the environment. When we do not see the outcomes of our lifestyles, we become oblivious to the consequences of our actions. Most of us have become so used to the convenience of putting our garbage outside to be collected that we no longer think about where it goes or what impact it is having on the environment. Are our bags of waste poisoning the soil or water somewhere? How much energy does it take to dispose of our refuse? Is our waste destroying the natural landscape? Those who live in urban and suburban areas can also take for granted the amount of energy we use on a daily basis. How is the heating or cooling of our homes having an impact on the resources we extract from the earth? If there is a limit to these resources, how are we changing our homes so that they become more efficient? Can we find ways to produce some of these resources—e.g., electricity through solar panels—so that we can become less reliant on mass-produced energy? We can also take for granted the fact that we have clean, running water. Are our household machines efficient in their use of water and energy? Do we know where our water comes from and are we using it judiciously? Is it a source that is being depleted rapidly or being contaminated by our consumption of it? Our modern homes have the potential to become microcosms of factory waste and destruction if we only take in the world's goods and convert them into pollutants or harmful sewage. All of these questions must be raised by citizens of God's kingdom if we are to take seriously the biblical mandate to tend and keep the land.

All of these issues address the fact that living in an urban or suburban center can sever us from the consequences of our actions and the reality that our lifestyles might be having an adverse effect on the world around us. And the larger and more complex the infrastructure of urban life becomes, the more likely we are to assume that someone else will take care of problems when they arise. We trust the "experts" to find solutions that will enable us to continue to live at the level of comfort and luxury that we have become accustomed to rather than considering what our personal responsibility is to change and adapt our lives in such a way that respects our place within the community of the natural world. While the movement from agrarian to urban life has not been without benefit to many, a great chasm has grown between a life once based on subsistence to one based on consumption, with little understanding of how our actions are affecting the world around us.

With the rise of urban life and the shift from individual to mass production, food becomes a commodity to be sold or traded on the market. Though food was sold and traded before the Industrial Revolution, the scale of such markets were minor in comparison. With the advent of farm machinery and factory labor the land was no longer central to the lives of a majority of the population and it began to be defined by its productivity and marketability. As corporate food producers developed methods for large-scale farming fewer and fewer people were required to work the land, and, indeed, those who stayed on the land could not compete with local and global agribusinesses. In some parts of the world farm land was concentrated into larger holdings and individual farmers grew more and more dependent on machines. These farmers were soon faced with the stark reality that debt, and possible bankruptcy, loomed behind every harvest. The increase in investment meant that the farmer was forced to forsake the agricultural practices he once knew in order to satisfy the drive of the economy. In this type of scenario, production takes precedence over the care and keeping of the land. Due to these and other developments, many were forced from the land as the weight of the economy shifted to urban centers while the life of the simple farmer moved toward extinction.

This type of mass production was not completely foreign to the ancient world, and in the Exodus narrative Egypt is the symbol of a relentless industrial machine that ignores the intrinsic dignity of humanity and abuses its natural resources for the sake progress. In Deut 4:20 Egypt is referred to as the "iron furnace," which is an appropriate description of the oppression and suffering that Pharaoh inflicted upon the massive Jewish population under his reign. The descendants of Jacob were subject to ruthless taskmasters and were forced to build storage cities (Exodus 1), but their tasks were made even more unbearable as Pharaoh's confrontation with Moses escalated. In a display of arbitrary tyranny and assertion of authority, Pharaoh strips the Jews from the land and casts them into the "iron furnace" of slavery where they become mere cogs in Egypt's tireless, cruel machine. Ellen Davis calls this "the biblical archetype of the industrial society: burning, ceaseless in its demand for slave labor (the cheapest fuel of the ancient industrial machines), consuming until it is itself consumed in the confrontation between divinized Pharaoh and the God of the Burning

Bush."[13] While the comparison to our contemporary industrial society is not exact, Egypt provides a biblical metaphor for the antithesis of God's purpose for his people and the land. Oppression and unbridled use of the earth's resources not only conflicts with God's desire for his people to worship him in freedom, but it also stands in opposition to his will for the Israelites to dwell in the land and to enjoy the abundance of its fertility. God's response to the cry of his people is, therefore, not only redemption *from* slavery in Egypt, but deliverance *to* worship and *to* a life of shalom in a land "flowing with milk and honey."

The Old Testament notion of salvation always assumes a connection to the soil and its produce. The agrarian life for the Israelites was, therefore, inseparable from covenant obedience. If the Israelites remained faithful in their cultic practice and maintained justice and love in their human relationships, then the land would provide in abundance. The land was the Lord's and Israel remained a tenant upon it so long as they held to the covenant. This relationship was characterized by a sense of humility, since the yield from the land was understood as a gift from God rather than the result of one's own efforts. The mystery of soil, water, sun, and organic growth was coupled with hard and laborious work, and in the end the Israelites could only watch, wait, and pray in silent wonder as their crops emerged from the land.

Festivals were instituted throughout the year to recall God's provision for the Israelites in both the past and the present, with a hope for the future. Sacrifices and offerings during these festivals were a way for the people to demonstrate their gratitude for the mercy they had received from God and there was no better way to demonstrate their appreciation than by giving up the first fruits—i.e., the most valuable portion—of their harvest. This was, in fact, what the Israelites were commanded to do upon first entering the Promised Land (Lev 23:9–21). They were to bring the first "sheaf" of the harvest to the priest as a sacrifice to God so that the rest of the crops could be released for ordinary use. Following this was a period of seven full Sabbaths (the festival of Shavuot) and then on the fiftieth day (Pentecost) a second offering of new wheat, baked into loaves, was presented to God. It is written that this festival is to be celebrated as a "statute forever in all your dwelling places throughout the land," which highlights the delicate balance between worship, sacrifice, and the cycles of growth and harvest that all have a deep significance in Israel's memory and recollection of God's salvation,

13. Davis, *Scripture, Culture, and Agriculture*, 68.

promise, and blessing. So critical is the relationship between salvation and soil that one could not properly worship in times of famine or draught. For salvation to be celebrated the land must play its role in bringing forth its yield so that, as an expression of thanksgiving, the Israelites might give back what ultimately comes from, and belongs to, God. Thinking back to Cain's punishment of being cut off from the land, we can understand how a Jew might have perceived the severity of his sentence as one stripped of life, worship, and salvation.

Contrary to this pattern of worship and sense of gratitude is the type of farming, commonly called "agribusiness," that dominates in certain countries today. Agribusiness treats the land as tool for production rather than as a partner in salvation. Instead of waiting patiently to watch the mystery of growth take place, the agribusiness uses an array of chemicals and fertilizers—and often genetically modified seed—to speed up production and to make farming as efficient as possible. The goal is to provide the maximum yield for minimal effort, but at what cost? While we have seen the ability of agribusiness to provide massive crops, we have also witnessed soil erosion and toxification, the increased use of fossil fuels, the destruction of genetically "pure" seed and increased homogenization. When our primary conception of the land moves from gift to resource—or from sacred to slave—we can begin to approach it with a sense of utilitarianism that values efficiency of production rather than partnership. We place ourselves above the natural harmonies and cycles of harvest and, instead, secure our existence by force and innovation. This is not to say that farmers throughout the centuries have not tried to manipulate creation in order to achieve better production, but the scale at which it is done today has never been seen in previous generations. A farmer may have isolated seeds from his best producing and most pest-resistant crops in the past, but this is not comparable to modern genetic modifications where genes from insects are spliced into seeds to make them pest resistant. And when the pests evolve and develop a resistance to the genetically modified crop, the seed is altered again and again. So the process has been since the 1980s in the U.S. when these modifications began to be implemented in farming, but where is it leading? Are we bordering on the edge of creating "super-pests" that will, one day, destroy all of our genetically modified crops?

Another significant factor contributing to our treatment of the land has been the intellectual developments associated with modernism. Up until the Enlightenment of the seventeenth century, the "pre-modern" perspective dominated Western history. This worldview might also be called "revelatory" since the emphasis is placed on knowledge through revelation or belief. Thus philosophy, reason, and science—or natural philosophy— were subject to faith in the pre-modern mind. One must believe in order to know, and Truth is absolute in the sense that it is the same for all human beings since it comes from God (or the gods). In contrast, the transition brought about by the "modern" views of the Enlightenment emphasized the discovery of truth through reason, rationalism, and scientific method. Modernity claimed that science could prove objective facts that are beyond dispute and, with the elevation of reason, faith was relegated to personal belief. Scientists such as Francis Bacon advocated that science be freed from the religious authority of the church since religion played no role in rational discovery and progress. Religion thus became good only for moral instruction, whereas science could "prove" specific facts about the world. This promoted the belief that one could observe the world through rational, objective eyes as if detached from the object being examined. By doing so, some scientists disengaged from their role *within* the divine drama of creation and cast themselves as spectators on the outside merely witnessing the acts of creation rather than participating in them. From this rationalist perspective the notion of mystery becomes associated with ignorance and superstition, and the sense of the sacred or transcendental in nature is lost.

With the advances of science and modern thought the natural world gradually becomes objectified and begins to lose its spiritual significance. The notion of the divine potter's fingerprints being impressed on the wonders of his creation is gone and the earth is desacralized. If we speak about God only with abstract or theoretical language he becomes the grand designer who is detached from intimacy, or relationship, with his creation. Gone is the God of Genesis—the artist who speaks the cosmos into being and breathes the breath of life into those who bear his divine image. Gone is the God who responds to Job in a poetic polemic that describes his active and intimate role within the order of the universe (Job 38–39). Gone is the God to whom all creation sings and to whom the psalmist enjoins us to praise in the company of angels and of all heaven and earth. And what we are given in exchange is an insipid, uninspired version of Ockham's clockmaker God—a God of omnipotence but void of relation, a God of power without love, and a God of technical design without beauty and artistry.

With the modern also emerged the secular, which was driven by reason and often anti-religious rational thought that severed humanity from its communion with the cosmos. The original community of God, creation, and humanity was rent in two with God and creation on one side as objects of empirical inquiry, and human beings on the other acting as autonomous, supra-mundane inquisitors. While it is difficult to pinpoint the exact moments where this type of individual autonomy took shape, it is clear that rationalism and the scientific method associated with modernity allowed humans to place themselves outside of the community of creation. No longer were we participants beneath the divine transcendence and activity of the living God, but we, in many ways, assumed the role of God and placed ourselves at the center of creation to direct its fate by our will. Norman Wirzba sums this up when he writes, "Whereas premodern cultures understood value to be embedded within the world, the modern mind separated fact and value, housing the former in an objective world and the latter in a form-giving subject. The sense of the world as creation, as ordered in terms of a divine plan, is largely gone."[14] Thus the secular mind produced by modernity fails to give proper regard to our susceptibility to the forces of life and death, but, rather, seeks to control and manipulate the environment as if we were somehow living above the earth and not within it.

Our modern world has created the illusion of autonomy. We believe ourselves to be above the processes of the earth and yet, if given the tools to cultivate a piece of land or tend to livestock, many of us would not be able to produce the basic needs required for life. We have been released from the "mundane" world of agrarianism to pursue the comforts of a life sheltered by technological advancements, but oftentimes this has been at our own peril and at the expense of the environment. Yet we have not only distanced ourselves from physical labor on the land, but we have also extricated ourselves from those basic elements of interdependence that foster human growth in patience, humility, attentiveness, perseverance, and care. Without knowledge of how we participate in the community of creation we can, knowingly or unknowingly, destroy the very thing that sustains us and gives us life. Berry argues, "There is, in practice, no such thing as autonomy. Practically speaking there is only a distinction between responsible and irresponsible dependence."[15] Biologically and historically, human beings have always shared interdependence with creation. To believe that we can somehow disengage ourselves from this relationship is to pretend that we are like gods, dependent on no one but ourselves. Yet if our culture is to

14. Wirzba, *The Paradise of God*, 70.
15. Berry, *The Unsettling of America*, 111.

hope for a vibrant and prosperous future it must be based on relationships of interdependence—with the land and with each other—that demonstrate cooperation within the economy of God's creation.

CREATING EDEN IN THE ELECTRONIC AGE

The focus of our discussion thus far has been concerned with the biblical mandate to care and keep the earth, especially in relation to the land and agrarianism. From the story of Cain, and other Old Testament passages, we have seen a narrative of interconnectedness between humanity and creation. The salvation of God's people and the land are indivisible. The earth rejoices when we live in obedience to God's will and reflect the image of his glory in our lives and in our communities. And when covenant love is practiced among God's people, the earth responds with an outpouring of abundance. Yet when human beings devour and oppress one another, and when they selfishly abuse the land for their own gain, the earth mourns and languishes. To the twenty-first-century rational thinker this may all seem like a quaint, childish belief reserved for the uneducated. History since the Industrial Revolution has demonstrated, they might argue, that no matter what our circumstances we have developed the ability to produce or extract the resources from the earth that we need for survival. Drought does not distract or hinder modern machinery. Storms and natural disasters prove to be minor inconveniences that can be overcome in next year's crop. Animals can be raised in protected, indoor factories with artificial light and growth-enhancing hormones. This utilitarian approach to the land and its resources, however, has already proven to have destructive consequences— as we noted above—and shows contempt not only for the creation but also for the Creator. This modern worldview might be best summed up as the desire to manipulate the material of creation through the power of human-built machines for the end goal of a manufactured paradise. Through the work of human hands the earth will be brought to perfection and subservience to human dominion. We will construct our own artificial Eden.

Citizens of the heavenly city, however, stand in opposition to the arrogance and mastery that drives the consumer city. Instead, they work towards establishing heaven on earth, and, according to the biblical witness, the sign of heaven is God's presence among his people. In ancient Israel God's glory dwelt in the tabernacle and then in the temple. If Israel was obedient, God promised to dwell in their midst and walk among them (Lev

26:11–12). Yet because of their disobedience, the curses of the covenant came upon them and they were stripped from their land by their enemies and were forced into captivity. Though God had not abandoned his people, his presence was no longer with them in the Promised Land and the writer of Leviticus makes the point of saying that in Israel's absence the land was finally allowed its Sabbath rest—the very rest that Israel never gave it because of their disobedience and greed (Lev 26:34–35). In post-exilic Israel the land remained firmly associated with the people's salvation, and we witness this also in later rabbinic tradition. Rabbi Yohanan said, "The Holy One, blessed be he, said, 'I shall not come into the heavenly Jerusalem until I enter the earthly Jerusalem.'"[16] Only when Israel responded in covenant obedience could the land be prepared for the arrival of God's glorious presence.

In the New Testament the presence of God among his people is made manifest through the incarnation. God becomes man and actually takes on the material world—he is born of the same dust of creation that all humanity shares. Whatever we might say about God's hiddenness and revelation in the Old Testament, in Christ we have the genuine form of the God-man. As John writes, "And the Word became flesh and dwelt among us, and we have seen his glory, glory as of the only Son from the Father, full of grace and truth" (John 1:14). In Christ we witness the inauguration of God's presence returning to his people on earth and this is further made manifest through Christ's death and resurrection. Jesus appears not as a ghost or apparition, but with a new body that somehow reflects the materiality of our future resurrection bodies. He is then raised in glory to be seated by the Father, but he has not left us on our own.

The next act in God's story of salvation comes in his presence being made known through the outpouring of the Holy Spirit in Acts 2. During Pentecost, a festival meant to celebrate God's salvation and abundant blessing in connection with the land, we see the beginnings of his glory going out to all peoples and all nations. As salvation in Christ continues to be proclaimed today, we remain in a time that is filled with God's presence through the Holy Spirit as his citizens establish his kingdom on earth, and yet we await Christ's return when his glory will be made manifest in its fullness. In this time of anticipation the Apostle Paul reminds us that, even as we long to experience the fullness of salvation, so too the earth groans in "labor pains" awaiting its own redemption. Paul speaks of the

16. *b. Ta'anit* 5a.

hope that, "the creation itself will be set free from its bondage to corruption and obtain the freedom of the glory of the children of God" (Rom 8:23). The land is still our partner in God's ultimate plan of salvation. And the final home of God, rather than being some ethereal place without shape or form, is here on earth among the material world that he has created and will re-create. John sees a vision of the new heaven and the new earth where God will dwell with his people (Rev 21:1–4), and there will be no need of a temple, or even light, because God's presence among us will be complete (Rev 21:22–23).

If we take this vision of salvation seriously, then we cannot be satisfied with our current culture that is driven towards the depletion and exhaustion of our natural resources for the sake of progress and convenience. Our lives and economies now should reflect the future kingdom that we anticipate. And if heaven is not some spiritually detached realm, but is, in fact, the transforming presence of God breaking through into our natural, biological world, then, as citizens of his kingdom, we are responsible for preparing the way for his coming. Thus, the proclamation of the good news of Christ is understood within the overarching narrative of creation's partnership with humanity in God's work of redemption. When we begin to grasp the profound mystery of the earth's participation in salvation we will recognize that we do not stand in opposition to, or above, creation. Instead, we work in collaboration with creation so that we might reveal God's glory now in preparation for the final revelation of his glory when Christ returns to dwell with humanity in all his fullness.

How do we, then, as citizens of the heavenly city, live in such a way that reflects God's glory through our treatment of the land? How can we demonstrate an appropriate interdependence in our relationship with creation that stands in opposition to the economy and ideals of the world? How can we begin to reorient ourselves towards a life of sustainability and care for creation? Rather than creating an extensive list of practical things we might do, we shall focus this final section on some simple paradigms that will, hopefully, provide a framework for how we can realign our lives with God's will through a biblical-theological lens that takes into account our role within creation. The temptation here might be to come up with hard and fast rules about what we may or may not do. But rather than turning the environmental question into a legalistic witch hunt that revolves around what type of car you drive or how often you fly, we shall try, instead, to recognize who we are as part of God's plan of salvation for the whole world, and how we might live as a witness to his salvation in the light of globalization today.

One issue that we raised, especially in relation to urban centers, is our contemporary attitude towards food and our being severed from the processes of food production. We noted that in agrarian cultures one's reliance on the land was a part of everyday life and fostered a spirit of humility since one knew that the production of food, the source of physical life, was something that existed beyond one's own creative powers. In contrast, the urban setting is dominated by symbols of human authority and control—cars, buses, trains, pavement, skyscrapers, streetlights, etc., all represent humanity's domination over the natural world. There is a diminished understanding of gift in the urban context when everything surrounding you shouts "Achieve! Acquire! Build! Conquer!" This is not, however, to say that urban centers are inherently bad or that they should be done away with all together as if we could return to some Edenic ideal. In fact, the biblical teaching is quite the opposite and we note that what began in the garden of God (Eden) ultimately will be consummated in the city of God (Rev 21:2). The point here is to illustrate the fact that we have lost the sense of gift when it comes to food since we have been dislocated from the land and have come to rely on our own power to manipulate the world around us. And it is here that we can turn to a biblical image that might help us regain an appropriate theology and practice concerning how we view our daily bread.

After having been miraculously delivered from the oppression of the Egyptians, and having passed through the waters to safety, the Israelites respond to God's awesome works by complaining that they will die in the desert for lack of food (Exod 16:1–4). God responds to their outcry by providing meat in the evening in the form of quail and a bread-like substance in the morning called *manna*. This flaky manna would appear on the ground after the morning dew had disappeared and the Israelites were commanded to gather an *omer* per person, per day, which was about two liters. On the day before the Sabbath they were allowed to gather double so that they would have enough on their day of rest. What is extraordinary about this gift is that those who gathered more had enough at the end of the day, while those who gathered less also had enough (Exod 16:17–18). Moses then commands them not to gather too much, as if they did not trust that God would continue to provide, since the manna would rot and be useless the following day. So important was the symbol of manna that God commanded Moses to take some of it and place it in a jar in the ark of the covenant (Exod 16:32–34; Heb 9:4). We are told that the manna ceased when the Israelites entered the Promised Land and ate of the first fruits of Canaan (Josh 5:12), but the sign of the manna remained forever present in their worship when the ark was placed in the Holy of Holies.

The significance of manna as an ever-present symbol among the Israelites cannot be underestimated. It is a constant reminder that, in their deliverance from Egyptian slavery, God never ceased to provide their daily bread and that all of their food is a gift from the hand of their savior. Even after they arrived in the Promised Land the Israelites were to remain totally dependent on God for their provision and were never to treat their harvests as if they had come by the work of their own hands. God is the giver of life—whether through miraculous manna on the ground or through the miracle of a seed that springs up from the earth—and all that comes from him is gift. This is what the Israelites were commanded to recall throughout all their generations; in the midst of death in the desert, God gave them the bread of life and taught them to trust in him as their source of life.

The same principle applies to Christians today in trusting that Christ, the "bread of life" who brings salvation to the world (John 6), is a gift given to us. Yet despite the fact that Christ fills out the form, or type, of salvation seen in the manna, and commands his followers not to work for food that perishes but "for food that endures to eternal life" (John 6:27), this does not mean that we are somehow transformed into spiritual beings who no longer require daily bread. Instead, Jesus reminds us that, in the economy of God's kingdom, we prioritize our trust in him first as the bread that gives eternal life and then as the one who provides bread to meet our physical needs (e.g., as we see in the feeding of the five thousand prior to Jesus's discourse in John 6). Jesus embodies the symbol of bread and sheds new light on the original meaning of the manna by declaring that he is the true bread from heaven who will bring salvation to the world. Thus he is the giver of bread for eternal life as well as the giver of bread for physical life. In both instances we notice that bread—whether spiritual or physical—is given to us by grace as a gift and is a symbol that remains firmly etched into the design of God's salvation.

The sign of manna might help us form some appropriate questions regarding how we treat the food we consume today. Do we think of our food as a product that is produced on an industrial scale? Is it just a commodity to be bought or sold? Is it something we take for granted and expect to be there at our command? Or do we think of food as a gift? Is it a sacred act to eat our daily bread with others in thanksgiving to the God who has provided it? In his meditation on Sabbath rest, Wirzba writes:

Manna is but one example among the many gifts we need to be sustained every day, gifts like clean air, photosynthesis, soil regeneration, energy, communal support. When we forget these gifts, or when we fail to see them as *gifts* and mistake them to be ours by right or by our own effort, we falsify who we are. We overlook the fact that our lives are everywhere maintained by a bewildering abundance of kindness and sacrifice.[17]

When we understand food as a gift we can begin to appreciate the giver of the gift as well as the processes behind what allows the gift to come into being. Rather than the product of machine-driven agribusiness, we can begin to appreciate the practice of working, watching, waiting, and standing in awe of the intricate web of creation that allows for life to spring up from the soil. We might recall the words of the evening Sabbath prayer in the Jewish tradition when bread and wine are placed on the table as a reminder of God's provision in the wilderness: "Blessed are you, Lord, our God, King of the universe who creates the fruit of the vine. . . . Blessed are you, Lord, our God, King of the universe who brings forth bread from the earth. Amen."

For those who have the opportunity to garden and grow their own food there is a daily reminder of how dependent we are on properly caring for the soil, for our reliance on sun, clean air, and water. Yet we can also develop an appreciation for what comes up in our local soil and the uniqueness of the food we eat by making an effort to purchase food produced near our homes throughout the different seasons of harvest. So often when we purchase products in grocery stores they have been shipped in from all over the world at a significant cost to the environment. Would it not heighten our awareness of our local environment if we were to make every effort to purchase food grown locally? This may be difficult for some and especially those dwelling in cities, but it may be possible as more fresh markets emerge and the opportunity to join farm cooperatives expands. Even if we cannot buy locally because of our circumstances we can still choose to buy products in the grocery store that have been produced regionally or nationally in an ethically appropriate way. In other instances, however, we might choose to buy particular items that are produced internationally if they are providing opportunities to farmers in developing economies and participate in fair trade standards.

Another lesson we might learn from the provision of manna is the practice of restraint in our consumption of food. The Israelites were not

17. Wirzba, *Living the Sabbath*, 35. See also Wirzba, *Food and Faith*, for further discussion on our relationship between faith, food, and the earth.

allowed to hoard or to eat excessively, but they lived on what they needed. When they gathered and ate they had neither too much nor too little and nothing was squandered. Like the New Testament fulfillment of the manna story, Jesus lets nothing go to waste when he feeds the five thousand but, instead, commands the disciples to gather up all that remained (John 6:1–14). Does our consumption of food reflect this same pattern? Do we value the gift of food so that none of it is thoughtlessly wasted? In both the U.S. and the UK obesity has risen significantly in the past decade and has become one of the greatest health risks to the current generation. This is not only due to the amount of food consumed but it is also the type of foods we consume on a daily basis that are heavily processed and contain high amounts of fat, preservatives, artificial coloring, and flavoring. Yet if we think of food as a gift, we might find it difficult to give thanks for the unknown, processed meat in our hamburger, the saturated fat in our french fries, and the artificial syrups in our soda before we dig in! Paul says that our bodies are temples of the Holy Spirit (1 Cor 6:19) and what we put in them should reflect what is healthy and sustaining. This is not meant to lead us to any particular diet, but, instead, it highlights the fact that when we consider our food as a gift we begin to think about where that gift has come from, how it was produced, how it will nourish us, and how we can consume it thankfully without having any of it go to waste.

Being grateful for the gift of food might also help us move away from eating thoughtlessly as we consider the potential outcomes of our choices. Would we eat certain types of meat if we knew how animals were raised and how they were slaughtered? Would we purchase certain fruits or vegetables if we knew that the workers who harvested them were being oppressed or treated unfairly? Would we eat certain grains if we knew that the manufacturing process was destroying the soil and poisoning the waters of local communities? While in principle we might agree with the notion of food as gift, it can be very difficult to determine where food comes from and how it was produced in a globalized economy. And so many of us—myself included—are tempted to give up because of the sheer complexity that lies behind food production. Yet this is the very crisis of our culture that must be addressed if we are to be faithful as citizens of God's kingdom. If society has gone astray and our culture has cut us off from the very source of our lives—and our partner in salvation—then it is up to the Christian citizen, in modeling a life based on the principles of the biblical texts, to reflect an alternative lifestyle that demonstrates thoughtful and thankful consumption of the food that God has provided.

Another principle for how we can live in harmony with the land is by considering, once again, the metaphor of the *oikonomia*, or the economy of the household. In chapter 4 we discussed the nature of good housekeeping, which requires non-exploitative relationships, mutuality, care for the weak, and the wise use of resources for the benefit of the whole family. In the household economy there is a sense of communal contribution for the sake of the whole. There is also a time for work, for (Sabbath) rest, and for celebration as we attune ourselves to the rhythms of the seasons throughout the year. If we recognize our role within creation as part of the household community we will soon take notice of the way we consume. If we are systematically destroying the earth's resources by our lifestyles and are making no effort to replenish, replace, or limit our use of those resources, then we are not living up to our responsibilities within the household. If our interests are in short-term wealth at the expense of the environment and those around us, then our personal achievements have neglected the needs of others in the family.

Food is also central to the life of the household. Gathering around the table to break bread with our relatives and neighbors is a sacred act in the celebration of God's gifts. Food is more than a product that fills our stomachs and fuels us to do more work. It is a symbol of our connection to the earth, to God's salvation, and to those around us. As living creatures we feed on other living organisms—as well as dead ones—that sustain us and allow us to survive. We are part of the food chain and our own bodies will someday return to the earth. As our ecosystem feels the strain of an increased world population, the local household needs to become more conscious of sustainability and the global need for crops, livestock, and aquaculture that are restored continually through sound agricultural practice.

The food producers of the world also need to survive economically and whether large or small, the local household can make an effort to support those who practice sustainable farming techniques that are beneficial to the environment. The quality of food can often reflect the quality of life and if the household is resigned to chemically processed, manufactured goods that have been produced at the expense of the land's health, then that family will lose out on the abundance God has promised through the earth. But if the household takes seriously the ecological, moral, and spiritual aspects of food production and consumption, they will grow attuned to the grace and mystery of life that is encompassed within the wider context of death, rebirth, and new life. The local home can, therefore, become a microcosm of the great feast of salvation that God has prepared for his people and for all of creation. To participate in this messianic banquet is to live and act as one who celebrates with the whole of creation. We are not the only ones who have been invited to the feast, but we are joined at the table by all that has been made by the hand of God. And it is at the banquet table that we eat and drink of the fruits of the land as a promise of the sign and manifestation of God's presence and blessing upon his people. When we treat the land with justice, responsibility, and care in the present we prepare the way for a returning King who delights in bringing freedom to his children and liberation to his creation.

As we seek to define an appropriate Christian response to our use of natural resources in a globalized world we come to the simple realization that we live and breathe as participants within the community of creation and that our interdependence with the land should be marked by humility, responsibility, and care. We have been called to take our place within the divine drama of salvation and this includes our involvement in the work of reconciliation and healing in our relationship towards God, in our relationship towards our neighbor, and in our relationship towards the land. A posture of independence and oppressive mastery has no place in the city of God, since it only breeds selfishness, isolation, and greed.

Cain was condemned and severed from the land for his murderous acts. For many his punishment was considered worse than a death sentence, but in today's culture we have voluntarily cut ourselves off from the land and often live as though we have little to do with the material world that sustains us and gives us life. Yet to recapture our calling within a globalized society and to enter into the promised Sabbath rest (Heb 4:9–11), we need to regain an understanding of our identity and vocation within the natural world. We cannot sustain humanity through the constant depletion of the earth's resources or the destruction of other species and their habitats for our own benefit. This does not mean that we should cease from keeping and tilling the earth, but it does mean that we do so in a manner that reflects the owner and king of the land. We also do not need to forsake scientific discovery or technological developments, but they can be utilized within a theological and ethical framework that recognizes our biological interdependence with the rest of creation. If salvation is meant to bring about wholeness and healing, then humanity must play its role amidst the complex ecosystem we live and breathe in each day. And if we live—no matter where we are—as thoughtful participants within the cosmic scope of God's salvation, we will begin to usher in the peace of Christ into our culture and bring about God's Sabbath rest for his people and for the land.

6 The Return from Nod

Attuning Our Lives to the Heavenly City

Cain said to the LORD, "My punishment is greater than I can bear. Behold, you have driven me today away from the ground, and from your face I shall be hidden. I shall be a fugitive and a wanderer on the earth, and whoever finds me will kill me." Then the LORD said to him, "Not so! If anyone kills Cain, vengeance shall be taken on him sevenfold." And the LORD put a mark on Cain, lest any who found him should attack him. Then Cain went away from the presence of the LORD and settled in the land of Nod, east of Eden.

—Genesis 4:13–16

Another significant change we face in a globalized society is our increased mobility through the advancements of transportation along with our use of communication and information technologies. We have high-speed trains, jets, and automobiles that can quickly and easily take us to parts of the world that would have taken weeks or months to get to in previous generations. We can pop into our cars to run a few errands and not think twice about driving twenty miles in an afternoon. Yet most of the time we spend in transit is in solitude. We go to the grocery store, the shopping mall, or the café by ourselves, and though we are surrounded by people we remain isolated from those around us. We experience a similar isolation when we travel and find ourselves in train stations, airports, or gas stations alongside the highway—we are present with others, but there is nothing that connects us to these places or to the people in them. Instead, we pass through like shadows without leaving a trace as we move on to our destinations. Yet despite our isolation from others who are physically around us, we can often try to retain a sense of connection through our mobile devices. Instead of entering into conversation with people around us, we can text our friends, update our status on social networking sites, or post pictures in hopes that others will comment on them. So while we might be disconnected from those physically present in the space we inhabit, we might seek relationship and connection to others through our phones or mobile devices in the virtual world.

I must confess that one of the more subtle pleasures that I enjoy in our technological age is the ability to remain connected to others wherever I am in the world. There is something that I find very satisfying about the anonymity of sitting on a train or at an airport thousands of miles from home and being able to video chat with my children, send texts to colleagues, post pictures of my trip online for my friends, or just put in my noise-cancelling headphones and listen to music. Yet amidst my pleasant dislocation from the world around me—while engrossed in my phone, iPad, or computer—I realize that I can begin to feel more comfortable engaging with my mobile device than with the person next to me. In fact, I have almost come to expect that people will not disturb me as I sit preoccupied with updating my Twitter account! I recognize, however, that in these places of transit I feel a sense of release from any type of relational responsibility to those around me and I have come to expect limited human communication in exchange for connecting to others online.

There is nothing inherently wrong with places of transit or carrying around our mobile devices to communicate with our friends and family. I would be the first to admit that I almost never travel without something that keeps me constantly connected to the Internet. Yet as we inhabit these places more frequently in our lives, and as we become more accustomed to relating to others through our mobile devices, we might question how this is affecting our ability to relate to those around us in a meaningful way. Are we becoming more comfortable in the isolation and anonymity we experience in the places we pass through each day? Are we happier to be communicating through our phone rather than conversing with someone face-to-face? One challenge a globalized society presents for us today is the temptation to tacitly accept this type of anonymous lifestyle, to disengage from relationship, and to turn, instead, to our mobile devices to feel as though we are linked to others. Yet the more we submit to a world governed by technology that can isolate us and prevent us from living in authentic relationships, the more we become like solitary wanderers through strange and unfamiliar lands, surrounded by others yet perpetually alone.

In the previous chapter we looked at our relationship to the land and its participation in God's covenant and salvation. We also noted that Cain was cursed from the land and was condemned to a life of wandering. No longer would he tend the earth and live by its fruit, but, instead, he would be an outcast with no home and destined to stagger about the earth for the rest of his days. We shall discuss the language of the curse in further detail below, but, for the moment, the nature of Cain's punishment is a fitting metaphor to describe what it can be like to live in today's consumer city— lost, without a sense of grounding or connection, longing for the stability of home and community, and seeking an experience of peace that exists when one is in right relationship with God, with oneself, and with one's neighbor. Cain is uprooted from the land and will wander aimlessly with the deep-seated anxiety of one who is vulnerable and exposed to the dangers of the world. In today's globalized society many aimlessly drift through transitory places only to feel a sense of displacement and isolation. They fear loneliness and the vulnerability that comes when one is disconnected from community. Like Cain's punishment, life in the consumer city can be one of ceaseless wandering without hope of ever finding rest.

In the following sections we shall look more closely at the increase of these transitory spaces in our globalized world and how we fill our time in these places trying to remain connected to others through social media and through our mobile devices. Then we shall explore what it means to attune our lives to the heavenly city and to create sacred spaces where people can live, grow, and experience the joy of God's kingdom. But before we look further at the response of the Christian citizen to this reality of the contemporary world, let us return to the concluding scene of our story to try to grasp the nature of Cain's destiny and God's final judgment.

We find the elder brother faced with a bleak future under the curse of his sentence and so he appeals to God one last time. Mark Twain once wrote sarcastically of Cain that "it was his misfortune to live in a dark age that knew not the beneficent Insanity Plea."[1] Though Cain does not plead insanity, he does offer a response to his judgment. It is unclear, however, whether his words are a sincere cry of repentance, or if they reflect the terror of a criminal who suddenly realizes the gravity of his punishment.

1. Fischer and Frank, *Mark Twain's Letters*, 392.

The phrase in v. 13a is slightly ambiguous since it could be translated either as "my punishment is too great to bear," or "my sin is too great to be forgiven," or even as a question "Is my sin too great to be forgiven?" In chapter 4 we mentioned that the Hebrew word for "bear, carry, lift" in v. 7 could refer to the "bearing away," or "forgiveness" of Cain's sin. The author uses the same word here in v. 13, but in this instance it seems to refer to the weight of sin that Cain cannot possibly endure. Thus the "bearing of sin" in this case probably refers to the guilt Cain experiences because of his offense. Yet if it is being used with the sense of "forgiveness," Cain's words could also be read as cry of hopelessness, knowing that his situation is irredeemable (i.e., his sin is so great that even God cannot forgive it). The author's clever wordplay leaves the passage open to interpretation and we can see from the ancient translators and commentators that some saw Cain as repentant while others did not.

The LXX translates Cain's response, "Too great is my guilt for me to be forgiven!" This seems to convey Cain's sense of despair at the thought of living under a permanent cloud of shame and condemnation. Though we cannot be certain, the Greek translator might be conveying the finality of God's judgment upon Cain and his acceptance of his future life as one who remains permanently cut off from grace. We find a similar translation in the Peshitta ("Too great is my offense to be forgiven!"), which also conveys the sense that Cain believes he is beyond God's mercy. Philo argues that Cain rejected his opportunity to repent because he had been so polluted by the murder of his brother (*Worse* 96). Likewise, Ephrem the Syrian contends that Cain was unapologetic for his crimes and actually pleaded with God to take his life so that no one would mock him (Ephrem read v. 14b as "let anyone who finds me kill me"). Some of the rabbis also concluded that Cain rejected God's reproof and went away like "one who shows the cloven hoof," that is, like a hypocrite.[2]

Not all of the rabbis, however, believed that Cain's situation was beyond hope. In many rabbinic commentaries Cain's reply was taken as an expression of repentance, though some questioned whether it was truly sincere or not.[3] In the translation of Tg. Ps.-J. we read:

> And Cain said before the Lord, "Much too great is my rebellion to bear, but you have the ability to forgive it. Behold, you have banished me this day from the face of the earth. But is it possible

2. *Gen. Rab.* 22.13.

3. See *b. Sanh.* 101b; *Gen. Rab.* 22:11; *Lev. Rab.* 10:5; *Deut. Rab.* 8:1; *PRE* 21.

that I shall hide from before you? And if I shall be a wanderer and
an exile upon the earth, then any righteous one that finds me will
kill me."

In this rendering Cain recognizes the depth and consequence of his actions, but, instead of despair, he appeals to the even greater depth of God's mercy. Cain appeals to the divine nature of the God who is "merciful and gracious, slow to anger, and abounding in steadfast love and faithfulness" (Exod 34:6). Another rabbinic text suggests a similar interpretation where Cain responds to God by asking, "Is my sin greater than that of the six hundred thousand who are destined to sin before you, yet you will pardon them?"[4] Yet another story recalls Cain's turning from his sins and, after he left God's presence rejoicing, bumping into Adam along the way. Adam asked what had happened and Cain responded, "I repented and am reconciled," to which Adam replied, "So great is the power of repentance and I did not know!"[5] The emphasis in these interpretations highlights the nature of God's forgiveness and the possibility of repentance for even the worst of sinners. Unlike the other translations mentioned above, which seem to emphasize sin and judgment, many of the rabbis seemed to read Cain's response in the light of human repentance, divine forgiveness, and reconciliation. We note that Cain is still cut off from the land and will be a wanderer and an exile, which recognizes the need for him to bear the consequences of his actions, but he will go out as one under the mercy and protection of God.

In a very different interpretation, Augustine viewed the earthly city's founder as irreparably cursed by God and, unfortunately, understood this as a clear condemnation of the Jews. He writes that the voice of the blood of Abel that cries out against Cain is the same as the blood of Christ that cries out against the Jews. He goes on to make a similar parallel:

> It is not, "Cursed is the earth," but, "Cursed art thou from the earth," which hath opened its mouth to receive thy brother's blood at thy hand. So the unbelieving people of the Jews is cursed from the earth, that is, from the Church, which in the confession of sins has opened its mouth to receive the blood shed for the remission of sins by the hand of the people that would not be under grace, but under the law.[6]

4. *b. Sanh.* 101b.
5. *Gen. Rab.* 22:13.
6. *Reply to Faustus*, XII, 10–11.

It is somewhat striking that Augustine so resolutely denounces the chosen people of God and considers them cursed and excluded from communion with Christ. While it is true that Paul understands the gospel in the light of those under grace or those under the curse of the Law (Romans 6; Galatians 3), Augustine's typological reading of Genesis 4 seems to overstep the boundaries of how we might apply Scripture—especially the Old Testament—in a contemporary context in the light of Jesus's life, death, and resurrection.

The nature of Cain's horrific future is conveyed through a simple alliteration in the Hebrew pronounced *na wa nod* ("a fugitive and a wanderer"). The words *na* ("trembling, shaking, wandering") and *nod* ("wandering, fleeing") can express either an external wandering or an internal restlessness. The general sense of God's statement seems to be that Cain is cursed to "shake/tremble" and "wander" throughout the earth like a man displaced, restless, and driven from place to place without ever being able to settle down. It is unlikely that the phrase was meant to symbolize the nomadic existence of Cain's ancestors—as some scholars have argued—but, rather, it conveys the inward unrest of the murderer who will never find peace. Here we are presented with a stark picture of what it means to be cast out from God's presence, to be displaced from the land, and to live under God's judgment. Those who remain cut off from God's grace will wander aimlessly through this life, never settling into the promised rest that comes with dwelling in the peace and forgiveness that he offers.

Modern Bible translations vary in their interpretations of v. 13. Above, the ESV uses the phrase "fugitive and a wanderer," which conveys the sense that Cain will become an outlaw, banished by God. Other versions provide their own nuance such as "a restless wanderer" (NIV), "a ceaseless wanderer" (JPS), "a vagrant and a wanderer" (NASB), "a fugitive and a vagabond" (NKJV), "a homeless wanderer" (TEV). All of these tend to emphasize the physical vagrancy that Cain will experience, but some ancient translators and interpreters highlighted Cain's inward suffering and unrest. The LXX writes that Cain will be "groaning and trembling" upon the earth. It seems that the Greek translator's use of "groaning and trembling" is an effort to highlight Cain's mental state of anguish that is externally displayed by trembling. The LXX translator might have viewed Cain's punishment as that of a displaced criminal, condemned to a lifetime of inner turmoil and suffering.

When Cain should have stood in fear and trembling before God in v. 9, he responded in proud defiance. Thus his punishment is that he will tremble and fear for the rest of his life. Other church fathers offer similar, less optimistic interpretations of Cain's punishment. John Chrysostom, in his sermon on Romans 8, wrote, "You [Cain] did not fear him (he would say) while alive, you will fear him therefore when dead. You did not tremble when on the point of thrusting with the sword. You will be seized, now the blood is shed, with a continual trembling" (*Homily on Romans 8*). In a similar manner, St. Basil described Cain's continual trembling and groaning as a sign of his body being deprived the steadiness of strength.

> Cain had made a bad use of the strength of his body, and so its vigour was destroyed, and it tottered and shook, and it was hard for him to lift meat and drink to his mouth, for after his impious conduct, his wicked hand was no longer allowed to minister to his body's needs. (*Letter CCLX*)

Since Cain used his physical power to overwhelm his brother, his strength would be stripped from him for the rest of his life. Philo also notes the psychological suffering of Cain's punishment and writes, "Such is the sorry life of the wretched man, a life to which have been allotted the more grievous of the four passions, fear and grief, the one identical with groaning, the other with trembling."[7]

In the translation above we saw that Tg. Ps.-J. interprets Cain's fate to be that of a "wanderer" and an "exile." In the context of a Jewish audience, the term "exile" would have evoked images of the devastation surrounding the Babylonian sacking of Jerusalem (587 B.C.E.), the desecration of the temple, and being taken into captivity away from the Promised Land. The word choice seems to indicate Tg. Ps.-J's desire to associate Cain's punishment with the theme of exile, as it is understood in the light of covenant disobedience. Cain's punishment of being banished from the land, and from God's presence, to wander the earth becomes a foreshadowing of the future disobedience of Israel. In Leviticus 26 we find similar language to Gen 4:11–14 where God warns the Israelites of what will happen if they break the covenant code and do not repent.

> I will set my face against you, and you shall be struck down before your enemies. Those who hate you shall rule over you, and you shall flee when none pursues you. And if in spite of this you will not listen to me, then I will discipline you again sevenfold for your sins, and I will break the pride of your power, and I will make your heavens like iron and your earth like bronze. And your strength

7. *Worse*, 119.

shall be spent in vain, for your land shall not yield its increase, and the trees of the land shall not yield their fruit. (Lev 26:17–20)

Though the words do not provide exact parallels to Genesis 4 in every instance, we can see that breaking God's law will bring about consequences such as God setting his face against his people (e.g., Cain being hidden from God's face), a sevenfold punishment (e.g., Cain's sevenfold punishment, which will be discussed below), and being cut off from the land that will no longer yield its fruit (e.g., Cain no longer being able to reap the land's harvest). Just as Cain was expelled for breaking the law by shedding innocent blood upon the earth, so too the Jews would be sent into exile for failing to obey the covenant commandments. Cain, therefore, becomes the archetype of those who suffer the covenant curses because of their disobedience and are sent into exile.

Yet despite this portrayal of Cain being sent into exile, there is still some question as to whether or not this should be understood as a purely negative consequence. In a commentary on Gen 4:14, 16 rabbi Judah said, "Exile atones for half of one's transgressions. To begin with, it is written, 'And I shall be a fugitive and a wanderer.' And afterward: 'And he dwelt in the land of wandering.'"[8] The rabbis argue that Cain's penalty was halved because later in v. 16 he is no longer called a "fugitive" or an "exile." They also argued that exile might not only reduce a person's sentence, but can potentially atone for all one's sins. Whether or not Cain's exile atoned for part, or all, of his sin in the minds of the Targum translators is unknown, but we see an important theme emerging in one stream of Jewish interpretation, which is that God's justice and punishment is never without mercy.[9]

THE MARK OF CAIN AND THE LAND OF NOD

Having traversed the contours of the Cain story—both in the original Hebrew and through the ancient interpreters—we finally come to the

8. *b. Sanh.* 37b. Cf. *Pesikta of R. Kahana* 24:11.

9. A similar theme also appears in the Targum translation of Hab 3:2: "Lord, I have heard the report of your strength and I was afraid! O Lord, your works are great, for you grant an extension of time to the wicked to see if they will return to your law; but they have not returned and they provoke before you in the midst of the years in which you have given them life. Therefore you will display your might in the midst of years, for you have promised to renew the world, to take vengeance on the wicked who have disregarded your *Memra;* but in the midst of your anger you will remember in mercy the righteous who do your will."

conclusion, which leaves us with the question of Cain's ultimate destiny and his standing before God. Before Cain is expelled to the east of Eden, however, God responds one more time and his words are not without ambiguity. The phrase "If anyone kills Cain, vengeance shall be taken on him sevenfold," seems fairly straightforward on the surface, but when we examine its precise meaning, things become less clear. The first question we might ask is who will kill Cain? At this point in the biblical story, the only other people who were alive were Adam and Eve. Some contend that Cain was thinking about Adam and Eve's future descendants (possibly Seth?) who would seek revenge, or maybe that he was afraid of being killed by wild animals.[10] In any case, we are not told who these potential killers might be, but we only know that Cain is afraid that someone will attack him during his life of wandering.

The second question we might ask is who will suffer the sevenfold vengeance? At first sight, the phrase seems to suggest that whoever kills Cain, that person—who did the killing—will be avenged. It is possible, however, to read the Hebrew with the sense that Cain will suffer a sevenfold punishment, or even that his penalty would be suspended for a period of time until someone killed him. Whoever it is that suffers the punishment, the final question is who will perform the actual act of retribution? Will the sevenfold punishment come directly from God or will divine retribution be enacted by some other means? If vengeance is carried out by God himself we are then faced with the question of why God would act on behalf of the world's first murderer in a manner that goes far beyond the Old Testament notion of an "eye for eye, tooth for tooth" (Deut 19:21; Matt 5:38).

The problem of the sevenfold vengeance was not missed by the translators and each provide their own interpretation. The LXX translates, "Not so! Anyone who kills Cain shall let loose seven acts of vengeance." This sounds quite different than the Hebrew and it is probable that the translator understood the verse to mean that the person who finally kills Cain will ultimately put an end to the seven "acts of vengeance" that God brought upon the elder brother for his crime. This understanding is found in the

10. It is at this point that many twentieth-century scholars argue that the story is, in fact, about Cain's descendants, the Kenite tribe, who were thought to have been marked by God's protection with some sort of sign. Thus anyone who killed a Kenite would receive a sevenfold vengeance from them. The problem with this argument is that it is nowhere apparent in the rest of the Old Testament that the Kenites ever displayed this type of brutality. It is also difficult to imagine that God would condone such morally offensive behavior on the part of Cain or his descendants.

apocryphal book *Testament of Benjamin* (7:3–5) where God inflicts seven vengeances upon Cain, which consist of one plague every hundred years. Some of the church fathers argued for a similar interpretation. John Chrysostom gave a sermon highlighting the seven sins of Cain, which he draws from each scene of the Genesis narrative (e.g., Cain envied Abel, he plotted murder, killed his brother, lied to God, etc.). He then contends that Cain's seven punishments correspond to each of his sins and that God's final judgment was to put a mark on Cain, which was "a mark of infamy declaring his guilt and shame to all that should see him."[11] Basil also wrote an extensive letter on the subject reflecting much of the same reasoning as Chrysostom regarding Cain's seven sins and seven punishments. He concludes that God would not let Cain die, "For to men suffering punishment, death is a gain, because it brings relief from their pain. But thy life shall be prolonged, that thy punishment may be made commensurate with thy sins."[12]

Jerome also struggled with the verse in his Latin translation. He wrote a letter to Pope Damasus who had inquired about the meaning of v. 15 and responded by saying that Cain would live until the seventh generation and that whoever killed him would free him from the tortures of his conscience.[13] He believed that the mark God had placed on Cain was a sign of mercy and that Cain would live under divine protection for seven generations, during which time he was given the opportunity to repent and be forgiven. Despite God's punishment, Jerome saw the hope of restoration, which is not unlike some of the Targum translations.

Tg. Ps.-J. contains the most positive conclusion to the story and provides a dramatic turn of events where Cain is transformed from the son of Satan to a child of God.

> And the Lord said to him, "Behold, then, anyone who kills Cain—for seven generations punishment will be exacted from him." And the Lord marked upon Cain's face a sign from the great and glorious name, so that anyone who found him would not kill him when he saw it. And Cain went out from before the Lord and dwelt in the land of the wandering of his exile that was made for him from former times in the garden of Eden.

The first thing to note is that the Hebrew "sevenfold" is understood as seven generations, which is the amount of time Cain will suffer under his curse.

11. Chrysostom, *Hom. in Gen.* 19:5.

12. Basil, *Letter* 260.

13. Jerome, *Letter* 36:2–9.

Other Jewish writings contain similar interpretations with the idea that Cain's punishment came to an end at the time of the flood in Genesis 6. The number (seven generations) was calculated by concluding that there were five generations from Cain to Lamech (Gen 4:18) and that, by the genealogy of Gen 5:28, Noah was Lamech's son. Noah's children were, therefore, the seventh generation from Cain before the flood.[14] Josephus followed the same line of reasoning and argued that after seven generations Cain's descendants would also suffer under God's judgment. "God, however, exempted him from the penalty merited by the murder, Cain having offered a sacrifice and therewith supplicated Him not to visit him too severely in His wrath; but He made him accursed and threatened to punish his posterity in the seventh generation" (*Ant.* 1:58).[15]

The second point to note in Tg. Ps.-J. is that the mark of Cain is a sign of reconciliation. We do not know what the mark on Cain's face was, but some speculate that it was either the divine name (YHWH) or possibly one of its letters. In either case, in Jewish tradition it was a most holy mark that conveyed divine protection and was only ever granted to those who were just and righteous.[16] In the Targum interpretation of the story we see the pattern of sin: punishment, repentance, grace. Even though Cain still had to serve out the terms of his sentence, he went out from the presence of God as one reconciled and covered by mercy.

Not all Jewish interpretations of the mark of Cain were positive. Other rabbis argued that the sign was leprosy that broke out on Cain's skin (cf. Exod 4:6–8), while others said that a horn grew out from his head. Another rabbi claimed that the sign was a dog that God gave Cain who would, apparently, bark to warn off would be attackers! Whatever the sign was, there was still some dispute as to it meaning. We know from the biblical text that it was meant to be a sign of protection, but some understood it as a negative sign to warn others while some saw it as a positive sign to encourage people to repent of their sins.[17]

14. Cf. *Gen. Rab.* 22:12; 23:4; 32:5.

15. *Tanh. (A) Bereshit* 11 tells another version of how Cain was killed after seven generations. "For one hundred and thirty years, Cain became an angel of death, wandering and roaming about, accursed. Lamech, his descendant in the seventh generation, who was blind, would go hunting led about by his young son. . . . One time the lad said to his father: 'I see some kind of beast in the distance.' Lamech sent his arrow in that direction, and Cain was slain."

16. Vermes, "The Targumic Versions," 119. In *Song Rab.* 4:12 §2 YHWH's name is inscribed upon the Israelite's swords, but when they sinned the name was erased.

17. For more on the historical artistic and literary interpretations of the mark of Cain, see Mellinkoff, *The Mark of Cain*, 22–80.

Cain is, however, cast out to the east of Eden where he is to dwell in a land called Nod. We mentioned above that the Hebrew *nod* means "wandering" and so Cain will, ironically, "settle down" in a land of wandering (we might wonder whether the biblical author is making a bit of a joke here regarding Cain's fate). It seems, however, that the narrative is not concerned about a particular geographic location called Nod, but, rather, the significance is that Cain's place of exile lies farther to the east of Eden and stands in contrast to the original garden of God. Eden signifies abundant life, fruitfulness, peace and safety, where God dwells with his people. Nod, by contrast, is a place of alienation from God where the land no longer gives its yield, where there is constant fear of attack, and where life is forever burdened by an unsettled restlessness. We can see, therefore, how Cain's punishment might have been understood as worse than death since he is condemned to a life deprived of stability, protection, and the chance for rest. Such an existence strips him of any space for creativity, relationship, community, and the ability to grow. The last we hear of Cain is in Gen 4:17 where he marries (we are not sure where she came from!) and has a child called Enoch who builds the first city.[18] Once again, the biblical text leaves us with more questions than answers. We might conclude that Cain did suffer a just punishment for killing his brother, but, by God's mercy, he was spared the full force of his sentence. He was allowed to settle and produced offspring, but we are left with the sense that wandering and restlessness will define the rest of his life.

The founder of the earthly city will never again experience the Sabbath rest that God had ordained from the beginning of creation (Gen 2:2–3). Instead, he will drift through life with no roots in the land and an inward unrest that will never afford him peace. Though he bears a sign of protection by God's mercy, his fate is marked by purposelessness and wandering. The land of Nod is a place of discord that stands in stark contrast to the original harmony of Eden. It is a place of transience and detachment that—at times—resembles the isolation offered by our technological age. Yet the promise of Eden remains for citizens of the heavenly city and it is a promise of Sabbath rest and attunement to the Spirit of God. Technology, travel, and communication will likely continue to dominate modern society, but the citizen of the heavenly city can find ways to live in such a world by cultivating God's rest in their own lives and by becoming instruments of peace that seek to create sacred spaces where the kingdom may be revealed.

---

18. It is also possible to read the text as Cain being the builder of the first city.

TECHNOLOGY, TRANSPORTATION, AND NON-PLACE

In the beginning of this chapter we talked about the sense of disconnect and isolation we can experience in our modern spaces and how we might be more tempted to connect to others through our phones than to those around us. We need not look further than a simple trip to the grocery store to see how this plays out.

We usually get into our cars, shut the doors, roll up the windows, turn on the heat or air-conditioning, play music, and drive along with others who are also sitting in their own enclosed worlds. We follow the signs along the way that tell us where we can or cannot go before we arrive at the parking lot where we exit the secluded haven of our cars and enter the store. While shopping, we search for the items that we need to fulfill the purpose of our trip. There is usually little, if any, engagement with other shoppers. We may, possibly, ask for help from a store worker, but even this is not to engage in relationship. Rather, it is to help us accomplish the task at hand. When our baskets are full we proceed to the checkout counter, which may or may not be overseen by an actual human being. If there is a cashier we have the opportunity for a brief encounter, but often times this is reduced to a simple "hello" and our attention is focused more on the electronic card reader that displays its commands and then tells us whether our payment has been accepted or rejected. When the transaction is complete, we exit the store back to the solitude of our vehicles and go home.

It might not be the grocery store, but there are an increasing amount of settings in our culture where human encounter has decreased and where people pass through in isolation without connecting to others in a meaningful way. French anthropologist Marc Augé would call these types of locations "non-places," or spaces that we inhabit on a temporary basis that have little to do with cultivating relationship. He argues that "place" can be defined as "relational, historical and concerned with identity" and traditionally refers to an area where people are in relationship and are connected to their historical past. For most of us our identities are formed and shaped in a traditional "place" where we live, interact, and grow with the communities that surround us.[19]

When we consider our trip to the grocery store, it was not long ago that the shops we frequented were "places" where people from the community gathered together in relationship with one another and shared a

19. Augé, *Non-places*, 77–78.

common history. Whether a person went to the market, the tailor, or the general store, they would have known the workers, or other shoppers, who were part of the larger community. Trips to the store would have been accompanied by communication and relational encounters rather than transactions that take place in personal isolation. This is not to say that these kinds of exchanges do not happen today—there might certainly be places where we shop and develop relationships with workers and with people who are a part of our communities—but these types of encounters have become less frequent in a mobile society dominated by technology.

Non-places, however, are not something new. There have always been places where people pass through without any historical or relational connection. The difference is that in the postmodern world—or "supermodernity" as Augé calls it—our increased mobility has often led to repeated impersonal encounters as we pass through these non-places and interact more with technology than with other human beings. Whether it is in a grocery store, café, airport, train station, hotel, etc., we can grow less accustomed to socializing with people and feel more at ease with reading computer screens. And as our networks of transportation grow, and we have greater opportunities for local and global mobility, we might question what effect our presence in these non-places is having on our identities and how we relate to others.

If our identity is traditionally shaped by our relational and historical connections within particular places, then one potential danger of inhabiting these non-places more frequently is that we can become accustomed to our own isolation and lack of personal interaction with others. As we pass in and out of non-places we leave no trace of who we are or any impact we have had. And the more we are situated in circumstances that promote our solitary individuality, and require communication with non-human mediation (e.g., machines, signs, computer screens, etc.), the greater potential we have to become alienated from relationship and from our connection to a sense of place. If we find ourselves constantly surrounded by the temporary and the fleeting in non-places, we may begin to lose a sense of what it means to be committed to and grounded in relationships over the long term.

It might be helpful to reflect for a moment on contemporary travel as we wrestle with the concept of our presence in non-places and how it might be affecting our lives. Whether we journey by car, plane, train, or boat, we pass through places momentarily and have no connection to them or the people around us. We experience a sense of solitude as we go through the queues, wait for our transport, or watch the world speed by through glass windows. The fleeting images around us blur together as we make our way to our destination. We might have our headphones on or spend our time reading or watching videos, but the person next to us has little meaning to our lives since they too are on their own individual journey to their own destination.

When we inhabit these places of transit we have no intention of grounding ourselves in their historical background or creating deep, lasting relationships with those around us. These non-places are devoid of what we might think of as organic thriving communities, but, rather, they are places that increase our isolation and promote our sense of transience. Augé writes:

> [A] person entering the space of non-place is relieved of his usual determinants. He becomes no more than what he does or experiences in the role of passenger, customer or driver . . . he tastes for a while—like anyone who is possessed—the passive joys of identity-loss and the more active pleasure of role-playing.[20]

Non-places can contribute to the temporary submission of our identities if we choose to passively obey the expectations placed on us without remembering who we are as human beings. And if we assume the role of customer—rather than human being—we can be tempted to disregard our relational accountability and our responsibility to society as a whole. Instead, as a customer, we become more concerned with transaction and contractual obedience—that is, if I do what I am told, and have paid my way, you (the company or whomever) are responsible to live up to your end of the agreement. The more we find ourselves in these settings and the more we submit to the role of the customer, the less we are concerned with the world around us, and we can find ourselves becoming satisfied in our own solitude and entitlement.

This disconnect not only occurs in the non-places of transit, but it can also happen when we reach our destinations. Imagine that you are going to take a road trip to see the Grand Canyon and while traveling down the highway you stop off at a gas station in some little town in Arizona. You might greet the cashier and ask for directions while you browse the spinning rack of postcards. For you—and for many others—the station is a non-place and is merely a stopping point along the way. In the store you

20. Ibid., 101.

might see something that alerts you to the fact that the town is renowned for its remarkable production of the state's largest cucumbers. Whatever it is, there are signs or markers around you that try to establish the historical significance of that place, but this is usually of passing interest as you make your way back to the car.

After some time you finally arrive at your destination. Along with many others who have come to stand in awe of this spectacular sight, you pull out your camera, pose for a picture, and then make your way home or on to the next tourist site, or maybe you stay in that area for a few days to relax. Whatever it is, you have no intention of being grounded historically or relationally in that place. And this is true of most of our journeys. Whether we travel to see the Eiffel Tower in Paris, or the Colosseum in Rome, our destinations are places we enjoy, places we consume, and then, when we are finished, we move on. This is not a criticism of travel or of non-places, but, rather, as we become a more mobile society, it presents us with a new reality regarding the places we inhabit and how our movement towards isolation and consumption in particular locations affects who we are as human beings and how we interact with those around us.

The more we dwell in non-place, the more comfortable we can feel with our anonymity—and with our role as customer—than with who we actually are. During excursions to the mall, service stations, grocery stores, fast food restaurants, or other non-places, we can forget temporarily the burdens of the past, the concerns of the day, or the fears of the future. We can distance ourselves from our lives and our responsibility to those we are in relationship with. We are free to put aside social obligations or caring for others as we quietly slip through non-places undetected and unknown. In some instances we not only assume our anonymity in these non-places, but it becomes the expectation of others. If you have ever sat next to someone having a phone conversation in a public place, you will know exactly what I mean. The person speaks loudly about their deep, personal issues and then proceeds to get into an argument right in front of you. Soon they repent, confess to their addiction, and then recall—at length—the abandonment they experienced in childhood. All the while you sit next to them pretending not to listen, but when they catch your eye they give you a look of disgust as if to say, "How dare you listen in on my private conversation!" For some there is an expectation that non-places require us to become invisible and discreet anonymity becomes our social obligation.

When we reflect on the characteristics of non-place in our postmodern world we get the sense that it is not far off from the biblical author's concept of the land of Nod where Cain would experience a life of wandering and disconnect. Cain was cut off from his previous relationships, from God's Sabbath rest, and from the peace, stability, and security that comes with being rooted in the land under God's protection. Like a fugitive and an exile, he lived his life in constant fear without the possibility of rooting himself in community. Despite the fact that the biblical narrative tells us that he lived in a city with his wife and son, we get the sense that he spent the remainder of his days wandering in his own personal isolation.

For Cain the land of Nod was a place of condemnation but, for us, wandering in isolation through non-places has become a common occurrence in our daily lives. And though Cain was likely tormented by his inability to be grounded in a particular place and community, we can happily inhabit our non-places with the aid of mobile technologies that provide an outlet for our temporary isolation and give us the sense of being connected to others. Despite the fact that we consider ourselves a wired generation—that is, always online and connected—is our use of technology in non-places another potential issue that affects how we relate to others? Are mobile devices and social media actually disconnecting us from our communities and hindering our ability to pause, listen, and communicate with someone face-to-face?

THE DISCONNECT OF A WIRED GENERATION

I recently met a friend for coffee and when we sat down at the café the first thing he did was place his phone on the table. Within a few minutes he had logged into his social networking site to inform everyone that he was having coffee with me at our specific location. Moments later he was distracted by a few replies that came back with greetings along with others who were in the area asking if they might join us. We had barely started a conversation by this time and I was beginning to think that my friend was more excited about the prospect of telling others about our meeting than he was actually was seeing me face-to-face! This made me wonder whether our exposure to non-place, and our use of technology in non-places, is diminishing our ability to engage with others in a meaningful way. Can we lay aside the overabundance of technology at our disposal and enter into the demands of authentic relationship where we listen, empathize, and communicate our feelings? Or are we being drawn to technologies that provide the illusion of companionship without requiring our real presence in another person's life?

In her book *Alone Together* Sherry Turkle discusses the effects of being tethered to technology and how, despite our physical absence, we feel that we can fulfill our responsibilities in relationship when we remain connected virtually. "Most of the time, we carry that technology with us. In fact, being alone can start to seem like a precondition for being together because it is easier to communicate if you can focus, without interruption, on your screen."[21] When we have continuous access to our virtual networks of relationships, moments of isolation with our devices become like places of refuge and the anonymity of non-place allows us to ignore others around us without a guilty conscience. We can begin to feel entitled to our solitude in public places and, as Turkle's title suggests, we find ourselves increasingly "alone together."

In her study, Turkle describes the generation of youth who are growing up in a networked culture where they are ceaselessly connected to others through their phones or mobile devices and through social media sites like Facebook. Some of the young people she interviewed had experienced so much communication fatigue that they said they would only "speak" online and would generally avoid face-to-face encounters at all costs. Even the thought of a phone call produced anxiety in many of them and most said that they would rather text than talk.[22] Others admitted to texting their parents on average fifteen to twenty times per day. This is on top of the hundreds of other texts they send and receive with their friends. For some, texting provided an outlet from the pain of loneliness while for others it had simply become part of their unrelenting social life. Still others appreciated the safety that they experienced behind a screen where they were physically alone, but felt connected to others.

Constant distraction, connection, and disconnection have become the norm for today's young people—and for many others as well—which makes us question what effect being constantly available to others without respite is having on our lives. What happens to a person who cannot disconnect? What happens to one's growth and social or spiritual maturity if there is no space or time to reflect, or when part of one's life is publicly displayed on the Internet for all to see?

21. Turkle, *Alone Together*, 155.
22. Ibid., 178–79.

One of the interesting insights from Turkle's study was how young people viewed themselves in real life as opposed to their online personae. She found that many students treated their social media profiles as an avatar of sorts, representing who they imagined themselves to be or who they wanted to be.[23] Every detail of their interaction on sites like Facebook had to be obsessively considered for fear that someone who did not know them might misjudge who they were. When they post things like their favorite music or movies, they might be more inclined to put down titles that they think will reflect something unique about their image online rather than what they really prefer. They might say certain things because they think they *should* say them in order to craft their online character. The nature of social media, however, forces them to do this all in short blasts of information and with simplified sound bites, which can take up hours throughout the day and can require an intense level of scrutiny.

For many students the maintenance of a Facebook profile led to emotional exhaustion consumed by the endless questioning of what picture to post, who to friend, what details to add or leave out, and how much of their personal lives they should reveal. Some experienced a constant sense of anxiety in having to mold and update their profiles every day. This sense of unease was only slightly relieved whey they were online and in control of their accounts. One high school student remarked that it was difficult to stop because all of his friends were online connecting to one another. Yet when he tried to limit his participation on Facebook he felt like he was being rude to his friends and that even doing the bare minimum left him completely depleted. In the end, he summed up his relationship with social media and the effort it takes to maintain one's online persona: "Stress. That's what it comes down to for me. It's just worry and stressing about it."[24]

Social media outlets offer low risk relationships where convenience and control take priority over emotional investment. We have the ability to develop multiple identities across the web where we can fluidly shift from persona to persona depending on how we feel on any given day. Each avatar contains some aspect of our identity, or who we desire to be, whether it is on a site like Facebook, or playing an online game, or in some other virtual community. Yet this fluidity and wandering between our different avatars has the potential to disrupt our ability to meet with one another face-to-face and to devote our full attention to nurturing a particular relationship.

23. Ibid., 179–86.
24. Ibid., 186.

When connected online we sense the presence of others, but those relationships are flattened and reduced to simplified text or images that will, potentially, remain online for the masses to see. We can end up with virtual lives that have very little to do with our physical lives and the possibility of not being able to reconcile the two. If we act one way in the virtual world, how will that affect the way we treat others in the physical world? Despite our ability to compartmentalize different aspects of our identity online, these will ultimately spill over into who we are in real life. If we hide behind our anonymity and are cruel or spiteful online, we will likely become the same in real life. And if we become so saturated and accustomed to terse, deliberately crafted textual encounters online, there is a likelihood that this is how we will interact with others in real life. Consequently, we will no longer have the emotional stamina to maintain meaningful, intentional engagements face-to-face.

Another consequence of placing our lives online is that we can feel the need to construct and shape our Internet persona for others. People begin to take into account the consequences of how their interactions, multimedia, likes, dislikes, etc., will reflect on their image, or the personal "brand" that they are trying to develop. This type of personal branding is becoming more common today as people develop greater followings on the Internet or try to increase their Internet presence. As with some of the students mentioned above, people can become more concerned with brand management on their social media sites rather than expressing their real thoughts or opinions. If someone wants to portray themselves as an artist, architect, food critic, pop star, political pundit, happy homemaker, or whatever else, they can contrive a character that might reflect their real life or an ideal of their persona—or possibly a mix of the two—with the hope that others will follow their posts or engage with them online. The more followers you have the more care you must take in managing your brand or how you present your online self to the rest of the world.

The difficulty with personal branding is that it can potentially restrict growth and the freedom to think, dream, and create. Our thoughts and ideas may be stunted over time as the communication of our lives is reduced to pithy texts, doctored pictures, or videos produced on a daily basis. We might do things, or say things, in relationships purely out of a motivation to maintain our public image. And if we do not keep up with the rapid flow of information, or if we are not churning out something new and cutting edge, then our brand will suffer and part of our online identity will suffer. People want to trust brands and feel a sense of security in knowing exactly what they will get in a certain product and how they will be perceived by using a certain product. If we are branding our lives online we can reduce ourselves to being yet another popular commodity and be conformed to living within the expectations that others place on that product.

The consumer city of today fosters a life of wandering through non-places where we are often left "alone together." Yet in our loneliness we have the lure of technology and the weight of our hope is placed on devices that provide the illusion of being connected in relationship, but, in reality, require little personal commitment. The more that we are drawn into these virtual connections, however, the greater our chances of getting caught up in the unrelenting demands of maintaining an online life and the less we feel inclined to meet with others face-to-face. We can brand ourselves on the Internet and yet lose a sense of who we are or who we are becoming. In the end, we can feel like Cain—caught in the land of wandering, surrounded by others, but trapped in isolation. In her conclusion Turkle writes:

> My own study of the networked life has left me thinking about intimacy—about being with people in person, hearing their voices and seeing their faces, trying to know their hearts. And it has left me thinking about solitude—the kind that refreshes and restores. Loneliness is failed solitude.[25]

Are we losing the ability to sustain intimate relationships because of technology and the spaces we inhabit?

Every human being has the need to be alone, to pause, to pray, and to resist the demands of the world that perpetually beckon us to respond. Jesus did not have to deal with a mobile phone buzzing and ringing incessantly, but as he traveled from place to place he was constantly mobbed by crowds who sought his healing touch, his love, and his compassion. Yet each day—from what we can glean from the gospels—he went off alone early in the morning to pray so that when he did meet the crowds he could hear their cries, respond to their needs, and engage each one face-to-face. He entered into non-place and transformed it into sacred space by extending the power and love of God to those whom he encountered. He attuned his life to the Spirit and no matter what cacophony surrounded him he reshaped the crude noises of the earthly city to blend perfectly with the harmonies of the symphony of heaven.

25. Ibid., 288.

ATTUNEMENT AND CREATING SACRED SPACES

When Cain was banished to the land of Nod he was condemned to a life of discord. He could no longer relate to God, he was severed from the land, and he feared others as he wandered about trembling and groaning. Everything about his punishment stands in direct antithesis to the covenant promises God made with his people—that he would always be in their midst, that they would dwell safely in a land of abundance, and that they would enjoy his Sabbath rest and communal peace. These two contrasting pictures give us a view of the choice we have between the heavenly city and the consumer city of our day. Yet the choice does not always seem so black and white because we are daily immersed in the dissonance of our culture and we can get caught up in rapid flow of the globalized world without realizing that we are being swept away from the path that leads to the experience of Christ's real presence in our midst. The witness of God's immanence in the world is everywhere around us but how we receive it, and how we attune our lives to it, is the ongoing challenge. Being a Christian citizen requires a person to retune their lives to the rhythms of the heavenly city. Cain staggered aimlessly without direction and purpose, but attunement to the Holy Spirit reorients us and awakens us to who we are and how we are bearing the image of Christ in the world.

The goal of the believer who lives in the heavenly city is the entire submission of one's life as an offering to God, which is completed by the totality of Christ's form and glory being impressed upon the believer. We do not pick and choose which parts of our lives should be submitted, as if Christ could come into only those places and fulfill his desires for us. That would be like asking that certain strings of an instrument be tuned while others are left out of tune. Despite the accordance of some strings, the dissonance of the entire instrument would remain. Instead, Christ comes to the believer to transform their entire image into his own, with each person bearing unique elements of his character and gifting. Every string is tuned in the believer by the Holy Spirit until they are completely attuned to the life of the Father and the Son. Von Balthasar writes:

> This holistic encounter from the outset both transcends every individual act of self-giving which springs from faith, hope and love and grounds it in a totality of both the subject and the object, in such a way that we are here both entitled and compelled to speak of Christian "attunement" to or "consonance" with God.[26]

26. Von Balthasar, *Glory of the Lord*, 1:242.

To be in concert with the rhythm and harmony of God is to live in tune with his Spirit and to be brought into the divine symphony of his entire creation. As his Spirit breathes over us we gradually let go of our own aspirations and desires as we accept the movement of his will drawing us into his presence and molding us into the work of the divine Artist.

Attunement to the pulse of the heavenly city is not something that happens all at once, but requires years of discipline. Just as someone learning to play an instrument must commit to hours upon hours of practice, so to the citizen of God's kingdom undertakes lifelong "lessons" which, like any practice, can seem tedious and difficult at times. We have already discussed some disciplines that help attune our lives to the kingdom—and, indeed, there are many that we have not touched on—but, in the light of what we have discussed above about the experience of isolation and loneliness in non-places, and being tethered to our mobile devices, we shall focus on prayer and solitude as an essential practice to reorient our lives to the rhythms of God's kingdom.

One consequence of inhabiting non-place and trying to maintain relationships through our phones or computers is that our ears can become dull to the sounds of the music of the heavenly city. We can wander off into a foggy haze unaware of the world around us and pass through places without the slightest inclination of witnessing—or participating in—what God might be doing. The scriptural narratives bear the weight of the divine presence bursting forth into the world and, despite the passing of thousands of years, the same is true today. The transcendence and immanence of God is fully present in our world and it is humanity's duty to respond. If God is trying to work through the narratives of our own lives, we can only be aware of his presence if we are actively listening. Jewish scholar Michael Fishbane writes, "Alertness is all. The call of God (through all expressions of reality) may everywhere break the veil of our daily stupor, and then natality overcomes mortality."[27] Yet this alertness can only occur if we are able to unplug from the pervasive din of the consumer city to rest and to pray before the living God.

In solitude and prayer we are awakened to the movement of the Holy Spirit in our lives and in the lives of those around us. Prayer is an act of defiance against the consumer city since it breaks us from the ordinary and opens our eyes to the needs of the world so that we might give rather than consume. It is often the case that we deliberately need to create breaks in

27. Fishbane, *Sacred Attunement*, xiii.

the ordinary routine of our daily lives to awaken us to the holy. Without the fractures that prayer engenders, we will fail to create sacred spaces for reflection. And if we fail to make time to contemplate the natural world and the spiritual realities of God's kingdom in our midst, then we will slowly relinquish our ability to grow. Fishbane writes, "The artistic imagination thus involves intentional acts of rupture, opening caesural spaces against our worldly habitude. In this way, it attempts to *cultivate the self.*"[28] Yet these "acts of rupture" are not only for the artist, they are for every citizen of the heavenly city who longs to break from the ordinary patterns of the world to bring about the cultivation of their soul.

When we commit ourselves to the practice of prayer and solitude we also begin to release ourselves from an unhealthy attachment to our devices. This is not true for everyone, but at times our technophilia and fascination with gadgets can be a subtle attempt to calm the restlessness in our hearts that Augustine said could only be stilled in God. Sometimes we might look to technology to alleviate our deepest fears of loneliness, isolation, or death. There are also times when we allow technology to blur the lines between the world of work and play, or between family and friends or our online identities. There are some, however, who might have no time for phones or computers and could care less about social networks and keeping up with the latest fads. Yet regardless of whether we might be addicted to technology or not, prayer and solitude are practices that allow the believer to stand before God in humility and vulnerability to lay aside anything that might interfere with one's whole identity being found in Christ. Prayer strips us of our egos, our aspirations, and desires and reduces the volume of own voices—as well as the clamor of the world—so that we might begin to hear his voice. And as we hear the whisperings of the Spirit, they begin to take root in our hearts; and we gradually ascend to the knowledge that our identity as children of God is not based on the size of our Internet following, or our ability maintain relationships through our phones or on social networking sites, but it is in Christ.

As we attune our lives to the heavenly city through prayer and solitude, we begin to create sacred spaces around us where the kingdom of God can break through. When we are alert to the divine presence in the world around us each day, we discover moments when God's glory might be displayed in our own lives and in the lives of others. And living in a globalized society that is increasingly characterized by non-place, the Christian

28. Ibid., 24.

citizen has the opportunity to transform these spaces into places marked by holiness rather than loneliness. Though there are many biblical narratives that demonstrate this type of transformation, I would like to look at one example in particular that illustrates this point.

In Acts 8 we are introduced to Philip who, like other persecuted believers, went out from Jerusalem after the stoning of Stephen to tell others about the good news of Christ. Philip performed many miracles while in the city of Samaria and he was soon joined by Peter and John, who prayed for the people to receive the Holy Spirit. After this encounter we are told that Philip received word from an angel of the Lord (Acts 8:26) and, though we are not told so in the text, we might presume that this message came during a time of prayer as Philip continued to attune his life to the rhythms of the Spirit. The angel tells Philip to go south along the road from Jerusalem to Gaza (Acts 8:27). He is not told to go to a village or to a city, but he is sent to a non-place, a road for travelers, traders, and sojourners. In the ancient world, journeys along highways could be very dangerous since one was exposed to the natural elements as well as bandits or thieves. Without the protection of a community traveling along an ancient road could prove to be a risky adventure. And, as if to highlight the fact that Philip is called to a desolate location, the author tells us that "this is a desert place" (Acts 8:26).

So Philip enters the non-place between Jerusalem and Gaza, probably wondering why in the world the Lord has brought him to such a lonely setting when he could have been in the city preaching. Then, in the distance, he sees something making its way down the dusty road from Jerusalem and the Spirit speaks to him, "Go over and join this chariot." It is a good thing that Philip did not have his noise-cancelling headphones on or he might have missed an opportunity to share the message of Christ! No, from the narrative we can tell that Philip is attuned to God's voice and hears the promptings of the Spirit and obeys. He runs alongside the chariot and begins to explain the words of the prophet Isaiah to the Ethiopian eunuch. And within a matter of moments he finds himself baptizing the man and welcoming him into the kingdom of God. In a place devoid of relationship, community, or historical grounding, Philip traveled through this non-place and, attuned to the voice of the Holy Spirit, he transformed a desert road into a sacred space. The narrative ends with Philip mysteriously being whisked away and we are told that the eunuch never saw him again (Acts 8:39). Yet in one brief moment Philip saw the veil being lifted before him.

He heard the symphony of God's kingdom and stepped in to play his part. In doing so he changed the course of one man's life and, as tradition tells, the lives of many others since the eunuch went back to Ethiopia to share the gospel with his people.

Christian citizens are invited into a life of transforming the places they inhabit into sacred space by attuning their lives to the Spirit through solitude and prayer. This might happen in the train, at the airport, in the grocery store, or in the local café. Wherever it is, when we are grounded in the discipline of prayer we become more attentive to the fractures created by the Spirit, which awaken us to our participation in bringing the glory of the Lord into the world. Oftentimes creating sacred space need not be dramatic, but can be as simple as offering a prayer for the stranger we pass on the street, or showing a sign of love to the people we encounter at the till, or even pausing to give thanks before our meals in a public setting. In each place we can offer the hope of Christ and ignite a small spark of light in the darkness.

Does this mean that we must turn off the music we listen to, put away our phones and computers, and stop updating our social networking sites? Each person must determine their own use of technology and how it is affecting their ability to relate to God and to others. This may not mean that we need to forsake our mobile devices altogether, but it does require us to seriously reflect on how technology and non-place are potentially hindering our attunement to the Spirit and our capacity to communicate with others and to create sacred spaced throughout our daily lives. For some this may be a serious issue, while for others it may not have any bearing at all. But no matter where we stand in relation to the technology and transit of our culture, a life that is rooted in prayer and solitude is essential to drown out the commotion of the world so that we might listen to and obey the voice of God.

Being attuned to the music of the heavenly city is a process that continues throughout one's life. The great Artist must tune and retune an instrument until the sound that resonates from it is perfect. As an instrument grows older it is constantly altered by its environment—heat, cold, humidity, dryness, light, or darkness all contribute to its changing tone. And the more that it is played, the more the artist must clean, tighten, loosen, and polish, so that it produces the resonance desired to bring forth its most beautiful sound. Von Balthasar writes, "So man has been tuned by God's breath to reflect and express the attunedness of matter and spirit, nature and God."[29] The tuning of our lives to the Spirit is a process that can be painful and frustrating at times, but the end result is a life that resonates with the deep love, grace, and joy of Christ for a fractured and suffering world.

Surrounded by the cacophony of the consumer city, we are constantly distracted from the music of the heavenly city. But as we continue to attune our lives to the Spirit we awaken to the joys of Christ's presence on earth and bring them to light for all to experience. Though the dissonance of human brokenness remains—and the brokenness of all creation (Romans 8)—we share in the universal longing to be set free from bondage to "obtain the freedom of the glory of children of God" (Rom 8:21). This freedom is the hallmark of citizens of the heavenly city.

29. Von Balthasar, *Glory of the Lord*, 1:101.

7 Conclusion

AUGUSTINE VIEWED THE KINGDOM of God on earth as a confrontation between two cities that would continue until the time of Christ's return. Those of the earthly city—like Cain—are consumed by self-love and seek independence, power, and possessions. Their end is only to bring about pain and brokenness in the world. Those of the heavenly city, however, seek the love of God and his justice and peace. They strive to bring about healing and the reconciliation of all humanity. Though the goal of the citizens in each city is vastly different, they continue to live side-by-side in the world and in the church. While the differences between citizens from both cities might not always appear on the surface, Augustine argued that true citizenship in God's kingdom is about the orientation of one's heart. Christians might not always do the things that God desires, but their lives are a series of steps and choices that are fundamentally moving them towards Christ and transforming them into his image.

Throughout history men and women have pursued lives of discipleship in the heavenly city. They came up against the social and moral challenges of their own day and responded with choices that reflected the truth of the gospel. They might have faced times of war, economic despair, outbreaks of disease, or times of peace, productivity, and prosperity. Whatever the circumstances, Christians throughout the centuries have continued to mediate on the words of Scripture in the light of their own cultural contexts as a way to hear God's voice anew and in order to best represent the gospel to those around them. And this is the task of today's Christian living in a globalized society.

Though it might not appear to be the best biblical text to speak to Christian citizenship in the modern Western world, the ancient story of Cain and Abel offers valuable themes that can still speak to our own times.

It is not just Cain and Abel, however, but the whole of Scripture that offers a collection of treasures for us to meditate on. And when we discover precious truths contained within it is our responsibility to share them, to hold them up to the light, and to allow them to reflect on the world around us. It is through this process of unveiling that the word of God has been revealed to us by the work of faithful men and women in the past. They have labored over the text and have offered their own interpretations and translations, which have opened up a historical conversation for us to enter into.

As we listen to how our predecessors communicated biblical truths in their own times, we can begin to formulate our own interpretations for how the gospel might speak to our culture today. While we must not sever ourselves from the faithful who have gone before us, at the same time, we also must not remain shackled to historic readings of Scripture that do not resonate with a contemporary audience. In many respects this book has tried to balance both by listening to voices from the past and from the present to understand how the biblical text can speak to a twenty-first-century Western context. Though we have just scratched the surface of the riches that await us in the biblical narratives, this simple story of Cain and Abel reveals the multilayers of truth contained in Scripture, and that even today God's Word remains "living and active, sharper than any two-edged sword" (Heb 4:12). And it is this Word that continues to speak to Christians living in an age dominated by technology and global integration.

At every point in history men and women are defined by their response to the crises of their age. For the Christian living in a twenty-first-century, globalized society there are broken and unjust systems that cannot be ignored. There are new forms of technology that have changed the way we communicate with one another and have revolutionized things like food production and the manufacturing of consumer goods. Yet whether it is social networking, participating in a global market economy, caring for the land, or inhabiting non-place, the current developments of our culture require us to reshape our understanding of what it means to be a disciple of Christ and how we are to proclaim the gospel afresh in this generation. If we resign ourselves to a response that may have been suitable for other historic times or places then we will fail to live up to the calling of attuning ourselves to the Spirit and creatively responding to the unique issues that confront us today. And if we will fail to respond with a fresh expression of faith we might leave a chasm of hopelessness for coming generations rather than offering a renewed vitality and enthusiasm for the work of ushering in the kingdom of God here on earth as it is in heaven.

"Am I My Brother's Keeper?"

The current crises of our society, which we have discussed in previous chapters, requires citizens of the heavenly city to step back from the road they are on, take a look at their maps (or their GPS-enabled device!), and re-plan their journey. If the world is steering us in the wrong direction we need not follow, but, rather, we can reorient ourselves to Christ, set out new paradigms for living as his followers, and discover new forms of commitment that will shape the vision for the future.

Throughout this book we have touched on some of the classic Christian disciplines and other ways in which we might address the crises of our world but we have, by no means, offered an exhaustive list. There are many other disciplines to be incorporated into our lives and there are also a host of other issues that we face today such as child slavery, child prostitution, poverty, poor education, lack of medical resources or clean water, which all require a Christian response. Yet as we establish new patterns of kingdom living in our daily routines, we will begin to pave the way for God's love, justice, and mercy to take hold in all aspects of our society. The hope is that we do not settle for generic solutions to the issues of our day, but, instead, we remain committed to the indispensable goal of bringing about the protection and preservation of the dignity that every human person deserves as one who bears the image of God (*imago Dei*). When citizens of the heavenly city are oriented towards Christ and take steps in the direction of loving God and loving neighbor—and gather in unity through the church—no matter what the crisis, Christ's presence will be made known through his people and signs of his kingdom will appear.

As we have noted throughout these chapters, living as a citizen of the heavenly city is a holistic endeavor. When God summons us, he calls us as *whole* people and he makes no distinction between what is earthly and what is spiritual. Every aspect of the Christian life is subject to the authority of Christ whether it is the prayers we offer, the food we eat, the clothes we purchase, how we care for creation, or even our use of social media or the Internet. We cannot compartmentalize our lives and think that our use of natural resources, or our time spent online or in the shopping mall, does not have the utmost significance in our growth as children of God. Everything we do either brings glory to God or it does not. And, in a globalized society, even the minor choices we make locally might have significant consequences globally in establishing the kingdom of God.

Augustine knew that no one lives in complete obedience to Jesus's commands, but that citizenship requires us to keep trying no matter how many times we fail. Orientation towards Christ is not about immediate maturity, but it is about the choices we make on a daily basis—whether big or small—that conform us to his image. C. S. Lewis sums this up when he writes:

> I would much rather say that every time you make a choice you are turning the central part of you, the part of you that chooses, into something a little different from what it was before. And taking your life as a whole, with all your innumerable choices, all your life long you are slowly turning this central thing either into a heavenly creature or into a hellish creature: either into a creature that is in harmony with God, and with other creatures, and with itself, or else into one that is in a state of war and hatred with God, and with its fellow creatures, and with itself. To be the one kind of creature is heaven: that is, it is joy and peace and knowledge and power. To be the other means madness, horror, idiocy, rage, impotence, and eternal loneliness. Each of us at each moment is progressing to the one state or the other.[1]

The Christian faith knows nothing about maintaining the status quo, but, rather, every choice we make shapes us, as Lewis says, into more heavenly creatures or more hellish ones. Are the decisions we make—even in the seemingly insignificant areas of our lives—directing us towards God or away from him? Not everyone progresses at the same rate, and we are not to judge those who are beginning their journeys with those who have traveled a long way or with those who have not yet begun. Instead, we must ask the more important question—how am I progressing towards establishing God's goodness, love, justice, and mercy in all areas of society through my daily choices? This means that we cannot be satisfied with simple, prescriptive solutions to the problems we face in a globalized society but, rather, we continue to listen attentively to the Holy Spirit no matter where we are in our faith journey and respond in a way that reflects the love and grace of God's kingdom.

This process of obedience to Christ in every aspect of our lives is traditionally called "sanctification," but it begins for one when the love of God awakens the heart and he or she turns away from the desires of the earthly city. The breath of the Spirit gives the new believer eyes to see and ears to hear the beauty of Christ in his infinite love. The senses are thus transformed to perceive God in oneself, in one's neighbor, and in the

---

1. Lewis, *Mere Christianity*, 92.

surrounding world. This illumination of the whole person's being is what the early church fathers called the *lumen fidei*, or the light of faith. "Faith is the light of God becoming luminous in man, for, in his triune intimacy, God is known only by God."[2] Through the gift of the Holy Spirit each believer is invited to participate in the Trinity, to experience Christ, and to approach the Father with childlike confidence.

This transformation does not come through anyone's own efforts, but is distinctly an act of grace by God. And when this transformation occurs, his light shines out from the heart of the believer to make known the glory of God through Christ (2 Cor 4:6). For the God who discloses himself to his children—and invites them into his divine fellowship—does not do so without also sending his children back out. As God's countenance is beheld *by* the believer, so too is it meant to be beheld *through* the believer. The radiance of divine freedom in the children of God cannot be hidden but, rather, it shines brightly drawing others from the cold and darkness into the warmth of its light.

When the light of faith grows in the believer, its luminosity cannot be contained and it will shed its light wherever it goes. Thus the light of faith ultimately brings about nothing less than the sanctification of all life. The word "sanctify" comes from the Latin root *sancta* ("holy") and essentially means to inject or infuse something with holiness. And this is the task set out for every follower of Christ—to infuse the world with his glory. The Christian citizen is, therefore, empowered with the mission of entering into the mundane and making it sacred by filling it with God's holiness. This means taking every aspect of daily life—no matter how ordinary or commonplace—and consecrating for his purpose.

We have looked at some of the transformations that have occurred in our culture because of globalization and the development of information technologies. In many instances we noted how the modern world has disconnected us from the land and from one another. We have seen how life in the consumer city can be one of consumption, isolation, and loneliness. It is up to Christian citizens, therefore, to reestablish the sacredness of connecting to others face-to-face and to seeking holiness in our relationship with the natural world of God's creation. They can model a life of attunement in a society of discord. In due time, however, there will be further challenges, and future generations will likely face even more difficult moral and ethical questions. And they too will have to search the Scriptures to find their own

2. von Balthasar, *Glory of the Lord*, 1:156.

responses. What remains consistent through time, however, is that citizens of God's kingdom continue in the sanctification of all life through Christ. When the Christian priority is to infuse all levels of culture and society with holiness, then the glory of God will be made know among all people.

Though we continue to watch and wait in hope for a coming king, we remain earth-bound, organic creatures, gifted with the light of faith and entrusted with the responsibility of bringing that light to the nations. The light that grows within continues to shine when we conform to patterns of love, justice, and mercy in every aspect of our lives. And as the heavenly city emerges among us we find it is no place of dull mediocrity, but is filled with celebration and beauty. We have been gifted with the ability to see the world through the eyes of Christ and to reformulate it through our creative capacities in language, the visual arts, and music. We can create beauty out of chaos and bring harmony and life where there is dissonance. And while we remain in a constant dynamic relationship with the physical world around us, we also infuse it with the glory of Christ and the spiritual realities of his presence through the Holy Spirit. No matter what advancements the world offers—whether in science, economics, agriculture, or information and communication technologies—when they are submitted to the rule of God's kingdom and used for the benefit of humanity, all things can be made beautiful by his citizens as they prepare the way for the coming king.

Suggestions For Further Study

BESIDES THE WORKS CITED in the book—which I would highly recommend—I wanted to add a few more texts, which I have found helpful in my research. This will not be an exhaustive list, but, rather, it provides a few more resources if you are interested in pursing any of these topics further. I will not cite any internet sources since, in most cases, a simple Google search will—hopefully—lead you down the right path.

GLOBALIZATION

Friedman, Thomas, L. *The Lexus and the Olive Tree*. New York: Farrar, Straus, and Giroux, 2000. An excellent overview from *The New York Times* foreign affairs columnist that deals with the social, economic, and cultural challenges of globalization.

Ritzer, George. *Globalization: A Basic Text*. Oxford: Wiley-Blackwell, 2010. A good introduction to the basic issues of globalization.

Stiglitz, Joseph. *Globalization and its Discontents*. New York: W. W. Norton & Company, 2003. A strong critique of globalization from a Nobel laureate in economics.

CONSUMERISM

Moore, Laurence, R. *Selling God: American Religion in the Marketplace of Culture*. Oxford: Oxford University Press, 1994. An interesting historical account of the relationship between religion and commercial culture.

Sennett, Richard. *The Craftsman*. New Haven: Yale University Press, 2008. Though not a book on consumerism per se, this is a thoughtful account of what it means to produce something meaningful in our work.

Stearns, Peter. *Consumerism in World History: The Global Transformation of Desire*. New York: Routledge, 2001. A good historical analysis of the origins of consumerism in Western society and also provides a broad overview of how consumerism has developed in other parts of the world.

There is an excellent series by Palgrave Macmillan publishers (London) called *Consumption and Public Life*. Many of these volumes contain essays on consumerism as it relates to politics, personal finance, fitness, advertising, the environment, and culture.

Economics and Global Trade

Britton, Andrew, and Peter Sedgwick. *Economic Theory and Christian Belief*. Bern: Peter Lang, 2003. A more academic look at economic theory and how it does, or does not, relate to Christian theology.

Stiglitz, Joseph, and Andrew Charlton. *Fair Trade For All: How Trade Can Promote Development*. Oxford: Oxford University Press, 2005. An insightful analysis on issues surrounding global trade and offers proposals for open markets that promote development in poorer nations.

Williams, Rowan, and Larry Elliott. *Crisis and Recovery: Ethics, Economics and Justice*. New York: Palgrave Macmillan, 2010. A collection of essays from specialists of widely differing backgrounds offering economic and theological responses to the financial meltdown of 2007.

Ecology, Environment, and Food

Brown, William P. *The Seven Pillars of Creation: The Bible, Science, and the Ecology of Wonder*. New York: Oxford University Press, 2010. An excellent comparison of the biblical creation accounts with contemporary scientific studies.

Fukuoka, Manasobu. *The Road Back to Nature: Regaining the Paradise Lost.* Translated by F. P. Metreaud. Tokyo: Japan Publications, Inc., 1987. Interesting insights from a spiritual Japanese farmer on how we treat the land and make peace with the earth.

Moltmann, Jürgen. *God in Creation: An Ecological Doctrine of Creation.* Translated by Margaret Kohl. London: SCM Press, 1985. A systematic theology of creation.

Muers, Rachel, and David Grumett, editors. *Eating and Believing: Interdisciplinary Perspectives on Vegetarianism and Theology.* London: T & T Clark, 2008. A collection of essays that cover theological, historical, and philosophical perspectives on eating.

Shuman, Joel, and L. Roger Owens, *Wendell Berry and Religion.* Lexington: University of Kentucky Press, 2009. A collection of essays on theological and environmental topics, which highlight themes from the life and work of Wendell Berry.

TECHNOLOGY AND SOCIAL MEDIA

Bauerline, Mark. *The Digital Divide: Arguments for and Against Facebook, Google, Texting, and the Age of Social Networking.* New York: Penguin Group, 2011. A collection of essays that reflect various opinions on the pros and cons of digital social culture. These touch on a wide range of topics from learning, to culture, to neuroscience.

Baym, Nancy. *Personal Connections in the Digital Age.* Malden, MA: Polity Press, 2010. A balanced account about the positive and negative effects of communication technologies on relationships.

Carr, Nicholas. *The Shallows: What the Internet is Doing to Our Brains.* New York: W. W. Norton & Company, 2011. A compelling account of the physiological effects the internet is having on our minds and on our intellectual and cultural growth.

Jackson, Maggie. *Distracted: The Erosion of Attention and the Coming Dark Age*. New York: Prometheus, 2008. A journalist's analysis of the detrimental effects of being constantly distracted by technology.

Bibliography

Anderson, H. 4 *Maccabees* in *The Old Testament Pseudepigrapha*. Edited by J. H. Charlesworth, 2 vols. New York: Doubleday, 1983.

Aristotle. *Aristotle: Nicomachean Ethics*. Translated by H. Rackham. Loeb Classical Library. Cambridge, MA: Harvard University Press, 1968.

———. *Aristotle: Politics*. Translated by H. Rackham. Loeb Classical Library. Cambridge, MA: Harvard University Press, 1967.

Augé, Marc. *Non-places: Introduction to an Anthropology of Supermodernity*. Translated by J. Howe. London: Verso, 1995.

Augustine, Saint, Bishop of Hippo. *City of God*. Translated by J. W. C. Wand. London, Oxford University Press, 1963.

———. *Confessions*. Translated by H. Chadwick. Oxford: Oxford University Press, 1991.

———. *Essential Sermons*. Translated by E. Hill. Edited by B. Ramsey. Hyde Park, NY: New City Press, 2007.

———. *Reply to Faustus*. In *A Select Library of Nicene and Post-Nicene Fathers of the Christian Church*. Edited by Philip Schaff and Henry Wace. Peabody, MA: Hendrickson, 1994.

Balthasar, von Hans Urs. *The Glory of the Lord: A Theological Aesthetics*. 1/7: *Seeing the Form*. Translated by E. Leiva-Merikakis. Edinburgh: T. & T. Clark, 1982.

Barth, Karl. *Church Dogmatics*. 1/3: *The Doctrine of Creation*. Translated by G. T. Thomson et al. Edinburgh: T. & T. Clark, 1936.

Bartor, A. "The 'Juridical Dialogue': A Literary-Judicial Pattern." *Vetus Testamentum* 53 (2003) 445–64.

Basil. *Epistles*. In *A Select Library of Nicene and Post-Nicene Fathers of the Christian Church: St. Basil: Letters and Select Works: Second Series*. Edited by Philip Schaff and Henry Wace. Peabody, MA: Hendrickson, 1994.

Bassler, J. M. "Cain and Abel in the Palestinian Targums: A Brief Note on an Old Controversy." *Journal for the Study of Judaism in the Persian, Hellenistic, and Roman Periods* 17 (1986) 56–64.

Bauckham, Richard. *Bible and Ecology*. London: Darton, Longman and Todd, 2010.

Bauman, Zygmunt. *Consuming Life*. Malden, MA: Polity Press, 2007.

———. *Liquid Modernity*. Malden, MA: Polity Press, 2000.

Berry, Wendell. *The Unsettling of America: Culture and Agriculture*. San Francisco: Sierra Club Books, 1977.

Braude, W. G. *Pesikta De Rab Kahana*. New York: Jewish Publication Society of America, 2002.

Brock, Sebastian. *The Bible in the Syriac Tradition*. 2nd ed. New Jersey: Gorgias, 2006.

Bibliography

Cavanaugh, William, T. *Being Consumed: Economics and Christian Desire*. Grand Rapids: Eerdmans, 2008.

Chrysostom, John. *Homilies on the Acts and the Epistle to the Romans*. In *A Select Library of Nicene and Post-Nicene Fathers of the Christian Church*. Edited by Philip Schaff and Henry Wace. Peabody, MA: Hendrickson, 1994.

————. *Homilies in Genesis*. In *A Select Library of Nicene and Post-Nicene Fathers of the Christian Church*. Edited by Philip Schaff and Henry Wace. Peabody, MA: Hendrickson, 1994.

Davis, Ellen. *Scripture, Culture, and Agriculture: An Agrarian Reading of the Bible*. Cambridge: Cambridge University Press, 2009.

Ephrem the Syrian. *Saint Ephrem's Commentary on Tatian's Diatessaron*. Translated by C. McCarthy. Journal of Semitic Studies Supplement 2. Oxford: Oxford University Press, 1993.

————. *Sancti Ephraem Syri Genesim et in Exodum commentarii. (Commentaries on Genesis and Exodus.)* Edited by R. M. Tonneau. CSCO 152/71. Louvain: Durbecq, 1955.

Fischer, V., and M. B. Frank. *Mark Twain's Letters, Volume 4: 1870–1871*. Berkeley: California University Press, 1995.

Fishbane, Michael. *Sacred Attunement: A Jewish Theology*. Chicago: University of Chicago Press, 2008.

Foster, Richard. *Celebration of Discipline*. New York: HarperCollins, 1978.

Gordon, Robert P. "'Couch' or 'Crouch'?": Genesis 4:7 and the Temptation of Cain." In *On Stone and Scroll: Essays in Honour of Graham Ivor Davies*, edited by J. K. Aitken, K. J. Dell, and B. A. Mastin, 195–210. Berlin: W. de Gruyter, 2011.

Harrison, P. "Having Dominion: Genesis and the Mastery of Nature." In *Environmental Stewardship: Critical Perspectives—Past and Present*, edited by R. J. Berry, 17–31. London: T. & T. Clark, 2006.

Irenaeus. *Against the Heresies. Ante-Nicene Christian Library: Translations of the Writings of the Fathers Down to A.D. 325*. Edited by Alexander Roberts and James Donaldson. Edinburgh: T. & T. Clark, 1867–1872.

Isenberg, S. "An Anti-Sadducee Polemic in the Palestinian Targum Tradition." *Harvard Theological Review* 63 (1970) 433–44.

Jerome. *Epistles*. In *A Select Library of Post-Nicene Fathers of the Christian Church: St. Jerome: Letters and Select Works: Second Series*. Edited by Phillip Schaff and Henry Wace. Peabody, MA: Hendrickson, 1994.

John Paul II. "Papal Address to Academy of Social Sciences." 27 April 2001. Online: http://www.zenit.org/article-1242?l=english.

Josephus. *Jewish Antiquities*. Loeb Classical Library. Translated by Ralph Marcus. Cambridge, MA: Harvard University Press, 1998.

Lewis, C. S. *Mere Christianity*. Fiftieth anniversary ed. London: HarperCollins, 2001.

Luther, Martin. "Sendbrief vom Dolmetschen." In *An den christlichen Adel deutscher Nation; Von der Freiheit eines Christenmenschen; Sendbrief vom Dolmetschen*. Edited by E. Kähler. Stuttgart: Reclam, 1970.

Mellinkoff, Ruth. *The Mark of Cain*. Berkeley: University of California Press, 1981.

Midrash Rabbah. Deuteronomy. Translated by J. Rabbinowitz. Edited by H. Freedman and Maurice Simo. London: Soncino, 1939.

————. *Genesis*. Translated by H. Freedman. Edited by H. Freedman and Maurice Simo. London: Soncino, 1939.

———. *Leviticus*. Translated by J. Israelstam. Edited by H. Freedman and Maurice Simo. London: Soncino, 1939.

Midrash Tanhuma-Yelammedenu. Translated by S. A. Berman. Hoboken, NJ: Ktav, 1996.

Miles, Margaret R. "Toward a New Asceticism." *The Christian Century* (1981) 1097–1101.

Moltmann, Jürgen. *Sun of Righteousness, Arise!: God's Future for Humanity and the Earth*. Translated by M. Kohl. Minneapolis: Augsburg Fortress, 2010.

Murray, R. *The Cosmic Covenant: Biblical Themes of Justice, Peace and the Integrity of Creation*. London: Sheed and Ward, 1992.

Neusner, Jacob. *The Talmud of Babylonia: An American Translation*. Atlanta: Scholars Press for Brown Judaic Studies, 1984–1995.

Niebuhr, Helmut Richard. *Christ and Culture*. New York: HarperCollins, 1951.

Paul VI. *Pastoral Constitution on Church in the Modern World*. Boston: Pauline Books & Media, 1965.

Philo. Translated by F. H. Colson and G. H. Whitaker. Loeb Classical Library. London: Heinemann, 1929–1962.

Pirke Rabi 'Eli'ezer. Translated and annotated with an introduction by G. Friedlander. New York: Hermon, 1970.

Ruskin, John. *Unto This Last*. Reprint, 2010 with an introduction by A. Hill. London: Pallas Athene, 1862.

Sacks, Jonathan. *The Home We Build Together: Recreating Society*. London: Continuum, 2007.

Scarlata, M. W. *Outside of Eden: Cain in the Ancient Versions of Gen. 4.1–16*. Library of Hebrew Bible/Old Testament Studies, 573. London: T. & T. Clark, 2012.

Sedgwick, P. H. *The Market Economy and Christian Ethics*. Cambridge: Cambridge University Press, 1999.

Segal, A. *Two Powers in Heaven*. Leiden: E. J. Brill, 1977.

Sen, Amartya. *On Ethics and Economics*. Oxford: Blackwell, 1988.

Tertullian. *On Patience* and *On the Flesh of Christ. Ante-Nicene Christian Library: Translations of the Writings of the Fathers Down to A.D. 325*. Edited by Alexander Roberts and James Donaldson. Edinburgh: T. & T. Clark, 1867–1872.

Turkle, Sherry. *Alone Together*. New York: Basic, 2011.

Tutu, Desmond. *No Future without Forgiveness*. New York: Doubleday, 1999.

Vermes, Geza. "The Targumic Versions of Gen. IV, 3–16." In *Post-biblical Jewish Studies*, 92–126, Studies in Judaism in Late Antiquity, 8; Leiden: E. J. Brill, 1975.

Volf, Miroslav. *Exclusion and Embrace: A Theological Exploration of Identity, Otherness and Reconciliation*. Nashville: Abingdon, 1996.

Westermann, Claus. *Genesis 1–11*. Translated by J. J. Scullion. Continental Commentary; Minneapolis: Fortress, 1994.

Willard, Dallas. *Spirit of the Disciplines*. New York: HarperCollins, 1991.

Williams, Rowan. "'Cloven Tongues': Theology and the Translation of the Scriptures." Wednesday 27 April 2011 in Great St Mary's, the University Church. Online: http://www.archbishopofcanterbury.org/articles.php/2023/cloven-tongues-theology-and-the-translation-of-the-scriptures.

White, L. "The Historical Roots of our Ecological Crisis." *Science* 155 (1967) 1203–7.

Wirzba, Norman. *Food and Faith: A Theology of Eating*. Cambridge: Cambridge University Press, 2010.

———. *Living the Sabbath: Discovering the Rhythms of Rest and Delight*. Grand Rapids: Brazos, 2006.

Bibliography

————. *The Paradise of God: Renewing Religion in an Ecological Age*. Oxford: Oxford University Press, 2003.

Wright, Christopher. *God's People in God's Land: Family, Land, and Property in the Old Testament*. Grand Rapids: Eerdmans, 1990.